How to Start a Microbrewery

Be Your Own Boss, Make Good Money, and Craft Beer That You and Others Love

By Cole Ferguson

© Copyright 2019 by Cole Ferguson - All rights reserved.

This content is provided with the sole purpose of providing relevant information on a specific topic for which every reasonable effort has been made to ensure that it is both accurate and reasonable.

Nevertheless, by purchasing this content, you consent to the fact that the author, as well as the publisher, are in no way experts on the topics contained herein, regardless of any claims as such that may be made within.

As such, any suggestions or recommendations that are made within are done so purely for entertainment value. It is recommended that you always consult a professional prior to undertaking any of the advice or techniques discussed within.

This is a legally binding declaration that is considered both valid and fair by both the Committee of Publishers Association and the American Bar Association and should be considered as legally binding within the United States.

The reproduction, transmission, and duplication of any of the content found herein, including any specific or extended information will be done as an illegal act regardless of the end form the information ultimately takes. This includes copied versions of the work both physical, digital and audio unless express consent of the Publisher is provided beforehand. Any additional rights reserved.

Furthermore, the information that can be found within the pages described forthwith shall be considered both accurate and truthful when it comes to the recounting of facts. As such, any use, correct or incorrect, of the provided information will render the Publisher free of responsibility as to the actions taken outside of their direct purview. Regardless, there are zero scenarios where the original author or the Publisher can be deemed liable in any fashion for any damages or hardships that may result from any of the information discussed herein.

Additionally, the information in the following pages is intended only for informational purposes and should thus be thought of as universal. As befitting its nature, it is presented without assurance regarding its prolonged validity or interim quality. Trademarks that are mentioned are done without written consent and can in no way be considered an endorsement from the trademark holder.

Table of Contents

Chapter 1: What is a Microbrewery and Why Should You Start One?..7

Chapter 2: Different Business Entities You Should Consider for Your Microbrewery...........21

Chapter 3: Permits and Other Requirements You'll Need in Order to Get Started...................39

Chapter 4: Drafting up A Winning Business Plan..59

Chapter 5: Different Equipment You'll Need....79

Chapter 6: How to Raise Capital for Your New Business Venture...108

Chapter 7: How to Avoid the Embarrassing Problem of Not Having Any Customers...........132

Chapter 8: Common Mistakes Even Experienced Brewers Make That Can Run You Out of Business...152

Introduction

Congratulations and thank you for getting this book!

The following chapters will discuss the process that is involved in starting a successful microbrewery.

This is meant to be a comprehensive guide that can enable you to start from scratch and create your own microbrewery without having to waste any resources attending seminars or taking online courses.

You will learn what microbreweries are, and why it can be beneficial for you to start one. You will discover the best business structure to use for your microbrewery, and you will get to know all the legal requirements that you need to meet before you can set up your brewing operation.

You will also learn how to come up with a winning business plan, and how you can go about executing that plan. You will learn about the different equipment that you will need for your microbrewery, and what you need to look out for to ensure that you don't overspend on the equipment.

You will also learn the different methods that you can use to raise capital for your new business venture.

After that, you will learn effective marketing techniques that can help you win over customers.

Finally, I will point out the mistakes that many people in your position have made so that you can learn to avoid them.

There are plenty of books on this subject on the market, thanks again for choosing this one! Every effort was made to ensure it is full of as much useful information as possible; please enjoy!

Chapter 1: What Is A Microbrewery, and Why Should You Start One?

You have probably heard about microbreweries, how they make unique beer, and how they appeal to many young drinkers these days, but have you considered starting one of your own?

If that is a business that you have thought about venturing into, you will learn everything you need to know about it here.

To get started, let's look at what a microbrewery is and why it might be a good idea for you to start one.

The difference between a microbrewery and a regular brewery

Before you can learn the intricacies of starting and operating a microbrewery, you first have to understand what it really is, and how it differs from other categories of breweries.

The main difference between a traditional brewery and a microbrewery has something to do with the scale of beer production (the prefix 'micro' implies that microbreweries are somewhat scaled-down versions of regular breweries).

The term 'microbrewery' has a specific legal implication. Some laws and regulations define different types of breweries for tax as well as consumer protection reasons.

In the U.S, the term microbrewery is used to refer to beer production companies that produce no more than 15 thousand barrels a year.

If your microbrewery exceeds the maximum beer production capacity as legally stipulated, then as the owner, you have a legal obligation to reclassify it as a regular brewery.

Let's take a look at the beer making entities that are larger than a microbrewery. The term 'brewery' is used to refer to one of two types of beer making entities.

It can mean a regional brewery (also called a regional craft brewery), which is an entity that produces between 15 thousand and 6 million barrels of beer every year.

If a brewery produces more than 6 million barrels of beer a year, it's called a 'large brewery.' So, regional craft beer manufacturers aren't the same as microbrewers because they make more than 15 thousand barrels per year.

It's also important to distinguish microbreweries from beer-making entities that are smaller. Nano-breweries are small versions of microbreweries.

Technically, there isn't a line that clearly distinguishes between the production capacities of microbreweries and Nano-breweries, but generally, the product scale of a Nano-brewery is quite small.

In fact, most Nano-breweries can be run by just one person. Microbreweries, on the other hand, need a sizable staff to keep things operational.

Another defining factor in identifying a microbrewery is that at least three quarters (75%) of all the beer produced at the premises of the microbrewery has to be sold off-site. If a microbrewery sells more than one-quarter of the beer it produces within its premises, it can technically be considered to be a 'brewpub.'

Brewpubs are getting more popular by the day, but there are still some states that don't permit the sale of beer within the premises where it's produced, so if you choose to invest in a microbrewery that doubles as a brewpub, you have to make sure that your state has legislation in place that allows the existence of such a business.

One important factor that distinguishes breweries from microbreweries is the question of who can own and operate the them. Legally, a microbrewery cannot be owned or operated by a big-name brewery.

This may seem odd in a society that encourages free trade, but there is a reason why this regulation was put in place. Without it, big beer companies would be opening small branches all over the place and calling them "microbreweries," and the honest microbrewers would have a difficult time competing.

So, if a big beer company starts a plant that produces less than 15 thousand barrels of beer a year, that doesn't count as a microbrewery—it's just an annex of a larger brewery.

Another key distinction to make is the difference between microbreweries and contract brewing companies.

Contract brewing companies are independent breweries that brew beer formulas which belong to other brewing or micro-brewing companies, in order to help those companies fulfill a surplus in the demand of their beer.

To work with such a business, you first have to incorporate your own brewing or micro-brewing business, and then sign a contract with them, asking them to brew a specific volume of beer using your formula and quality control measures. They will then package the beer in your bottles, and give it to you to sell and distribute.

Some people have used this method when venturing into the micro-brewing business, but it is quite risky. If you project a high demand for your beer, but if your beer unfortunately doesn't sell, you will still be on the hook to pay the contract brewer.

It's better to have a micro-brewing facility that produces all the beer you need so you don't have to outsource the brewing process. Still, if you account for all the risks, this could be a great way to get started in micro-brewing before you buy your own equipment.

It's important to go into the micro-brewing business while understanding that there is a legal cap to how much you can produce.

Many people assume that the micro-brewing business is very scalable, and they go into it expecting to bring in huge profits, but in the quest to expand, their brand loses its identity.

You have to understand that if you are running a microbrewery, your aim is not to outsell a big beer company and to become the most popular beer across the country–your aim is to make a unique beer that appeals to niche consumers with a very specific taste.

Instead of going for mass appeal, you are trying to make a few unique brews under your brand, and you are hoping that your brand will become popular among drinkers within a limited geographical region and that they will appreciate the personal touch that you put into your beer over the mass produced beer from larger companies.

The benefits of starting your own microbrewery business

Now that you understand what microbreweries are and how they differ from other types of breweries, you have to understand why starting a microbrewery might be a good business venture for you.

Here are some of the main benefits of starting your own microbrewery business:

The first benefit of starting a microbrewery is that you get to do something that big breweries do without incurring high startup costs.

The actual cost of starting a microbrewery differs depending on your production capacity, the location of your microbrewery (the location determines how much you pay in terms of rent and utilities), and other capital costs.

On average, the startup cost of a microbrewery is a fraction of what it costs to start a full-fledged brewery.

Thanks to the competitive nature of the industry, manufacturers are continuously producing affordable brewing equipment, so you no longer have to worry about getting expensive and limited options when buying brewing tanks and other equipment.

Researchers have found that the startup cost of a microbrewery can be anywhere between $100,000 on the lower end and one million on the upper end of the spectrum, so if you are resourceful and well organized, you could own your own microbrewery for much less than it would cost you to start a restaurant.

In fact, compared to most other types of lucrative companies that you can start, the startup cost of a microbrewery is fairly low.

When you have a microbrewery of your own, you get to explore your passion and your creativity as you experiment with different beer recipes and create your own formulas. Even if you don't consider the potential for profit, running a microbrewery can be rewarding on its own.

As you make specialty beer, and as you adjust your ingredients to get your desired outcome, you will come up with a lot of great batches, and you may just find the secret recipe that could become the next bestselling brew.

The thrill of experimenting can be intoxicating by itself. We all have a mad scientist inside of us, and having your own microbrewery allows you to bring yours out.

Another benefit of micro-brewing is that it appeals to a young consumer base that keeps growing by the day, and this means that there is a great potential for profitability, no matter how stiff the competition gets.

The sale of mass-produced beer has stagnated over the past few years, but the sale of craft beers and specialty beers has been increasing steadily.

This means that beer drinkers are getting more and more adventurous, and they are opting for craft beers instead of beers from large companies.

There are lots of reasons why the average millennial beer drinker would much rather have a craft beer than a regular beer. For starters, microbrewery beer has a great taste.

Beer from large manufacturers tends to have a somewhat drab taste because those companies focus on maximizing production capacity and profitability, rather then ensuring that each batch they brew is full of flavor.

That means that while the beer from big companies has a generic taste, the beer from microbreweries has a strong taste and is extremely flavorful.

Also, there is the aspect of variety. Microbreweries tend to put out a variety of products from which consumers can pick their favorite, so they are not forced to drink the same beer over and over.

There is also the aspect of freshness which makes some drinkers prefer the beer from microbreweries over the beer produced by major breweries.

Microbreweries tend to make beer in small batches, and they offload those batches fairly quickly, so the beer doesn't stay on the shelf for too long.

Also, the vast majority of the beer produced by any microbrewery is consumed within a limited geographical region, so it doesn't have to travel over long distances.

That means that microbrewery beer is consumed while it's still fresh.

By comparison, beer from large breweries has to be stored for a long time or transported over long distances, which means that it deteriorates over time due to exposure to light, bacteria, or even air.

There are niche consumers who understand the fact that microbrewery beer which has been produced recently is better tasting than beer which left the factory a few months ago.

These consumers are willing to buy your microbrewery beer, and they'll even pay you a premium for it.

Another advantage of running a microbrewery is that you can produce beer that is completely made of natural ingredients and is better health-wise compared to beer from larger breweries.

There is an ongoing trend, especially among younger consumers, to opt for products that are "organic," "healthy," or "artisanal," and running a microbrewery allows you to market your beer as all of those things.

When beer is mass-produced, there are lots of unhealthy preservatives that are added to increase its shelf life, and if you are making a microbrewery beer, you can forgo those preservatives because you don't plan on keeping your beer on the shelf for long.

You can eliminate all the artificial constituents from your beer and create a completely organic brew, and your consumers will reward you for it.

Another main advantage of running a microbrewery is that you have a lot of flexibility when it comes to pricing your beer.

You can price your product much higher than the products from large-scale beer makers, and you can make a fairly large profit from your brew, especially if you come up with a great craft beer recipe.

As I have already mentioned, there are sophisticated young consumers who are willing to pay more for a high-quality brew, and if you are good enough, your beer can be a big hit with that demographic.

Conversely, you can price your beer much lower than average and still generate a profit, especially if you focus on lowering your brewing and packaging costs.

When you start your microbrewery, initially as you are trying to gain in popularity, you can produce beer at a low cost, package it in kegs, and sell it to local pubs, where it can be sold to drinkers at a special low price, and you may still be able to make a significant profit.

Once word gets around about your beer, you may then improve its packaging (e.g., using bottles or cans), increase its price, and make an even bigger profit.

The microbrewery business and being your own boss

The greatest advantage of running your own microbrewery is that you get to be your own boss. You hear people say that when you are an entrepreneur, you are your own boss, but many of them fail to explain exactly what that means.

There are very many benefits of being your own boss, especially in the context of operating a microbrewery.

First, you will be in control of how many hours you work. When you have a fully operational microbrewery, you will have a few people on your payroll to perform specific functions at the microbrewery, and other than that, many of the other functions at the microbrewery will be fully automated.

That means that you don't have to break your back working endless hours just to produce the quantity of beer you want. After you have set up your brewery and everything is running smoothly, you can work as few or as many hours as you want; the most important thing is that it will be your choice.

If you are truly passionate about your brewing craft, you will spend a lot of time experimenting with different recipes, but you will be doing it for fun, not because someone else is obligating you to do it. As long as you have things in order, you can be certain that your brewery will still be running smoothly even if you take some time off in the middle of the week to do something you enjoy.

Once you have created the right recipes and you have set out a production plan, you don't even have to come into work. Your staff should be able to do their jobs and to create a beer that meets your quality control standards without you looking over their shoulders all of the time.

Being your own boss also means that you will be in control of how much you can make as you run your microbrewery. As the owner of the microbrewery, you get to keep all the profits from your business after paying your employees, covering operational costs, and paying your taxes.

Even though breweries are some of the most taxed businesses, you can still generate a sizable profit from your business to live comfortably or even to be truly wealthy.

The key factor here is that you have autonomy as the owner of your business, so you aren't limited to a predetermined salary.

If you have a job, the harder you work, the richer your employer gets, and you remain in the same position financially. If you have a microbrewery, you are the boss, so the harder you or your employees work, the richer you become.

Chapter 2: Different Business Entities You Should Consider for Your Microbrewery

One of the first things you will do as you start your microbrewery is to choose the kind of business structure that you want for your microbrewery.

There are usually several things that you need to keep in mind when selecting a structure for your business, but for our purposes, we will only look at the factors that apply to micro-brewing.

The first thing you have to think about is the level of control that you wish to have over your microbrewery in the long-run.

Some structures allow you to have unilateral control over the business, while other structures are designed to ensure that you are answerable to people like investors and shareholders.

Whatever structure you pick, you have to make sure that it gives you considerable influence over your company so that you don't easily lose it to someone else, or you don't end up in a situation where another person is bossing you around.

The second thing you need to consider as you select the right business structure for your microbrewery is the amount of liability that you are willing to shoulder as a result of the operations of that business.

Some business structures open you up to liability in case of injuries at your microbrewery or if someone gets sick as a result of consuming your brew.

It's advisable that you pick a company structure that limits your liability so that if something goes wrong with the brewery, your personal assets don't have to be put at risk.

You also have to think about the cost that you will incur in the process of forming your company. Different business structures require different procedures during their formation, and that means that the costs that are involved at that stage are also different.

The more complex the business structure, the more you will have to pay in terms of fees and permits, as well as hiring lawyers or accountants. If the structure is simple enough, you may not even need outside help to create the business— you can just file a few documents with the county and state offices, and you are done.

That doesn't mean that you have to go for the cheapest business structure out there. Instead, you should find one that strikes the best balance between initial cost and the value it offers you in the long-run.

Another thing you have to think about when selecting a business structure is the flexibility that it offers you, and the needs that may arise in the future.

For example, if you intend to expand your business in the future, you have to select a structure that allows you to scale up in various ways, including by hiring new employees.

Microbreweries have an upper limit when it comes to scalability (remember that they can only produce 15 thousand barrels of beer per year), but that doesn't mean that you should disregard the aspect of scalability all together.

If you have a little starting capital that allows you to set up a fairly small operation, to begin with, there is always a chance that you could scale up your business. There is enough room for expansion even within the 15-thousand-barrel limit, so you have to make sure that your business structure takes that fact into account.

If you select the wrong business structure and then you end up deciding to expand it, you could face some legal penalties.

There is also a chance that in the long-term, you might want to upgrade your microbrewery into a craft brewery, so if that is your goal, you should make sure that you start your business with a structure that will make it easy for you to restructure it should the need arise in the future.

You also have to think about the tax implication of the business structure that you have selected. The business structure you have picked determines to a large extent the amount of tax that you have to pay.

Beer making companies are some of the most taxed entities in most jurisdictions around the world because of "sin tax" (this is a special kind of tax rate that is levied on products that are deemed to be detrimental to the health of consumers, or the environment.

The intention of such a tax is to offset the harm done by a particular industry by channeling a fraction of its profit into doing some social good). Beer drinking is seen as a vice by many state governments and the federal government, so the tax is higher than that levied on most other consumer products.

That means that in order to maintain a decent profit margin, you have to pick a structure that minimizes your tax obligation. This requires an understanding of federal tax laws, as well as state and local government laws.

You have to weigh the tax benefits of each structure with the other benefits that the structure has to offer and then select the option that offers you the maximum utility.

You also have to think about the tasks that you will be dealing with from an administrative standpoint. Your primary focus should be creating high-quality and unique beer, not handling the paperwork.

Some business structures require a lot of record keeping, and that means that you will turn into a paper pusher instead of a real brewer.

If you are running a business (whether it's a microbrewery or any other kind of business) it's expected that you will have to perform some administrative functions, but don't go for a business structure that ends up burying you in a mountain of useless paperwork.

Micro-brewing is supposed to be fun, and too much paperwork can take the joy out of it. However, as a point of caution, no matter what business structure you pick, make sure that you do all the required paperwork because, without it, you could end up in unforeseen legal jeopardy.

At the moment that you are setting up your business, you also have to think about how it's going to end. This may seem like the wrong time to think about the end, but it is necessary.

What happens when you leave the microbrewery (whether you have to dissolve it a few months later, or you have to retire from managing it 50 years later)?

If the microbrewery is important to your family's financial future, you have to structure it in such a way that it continues to exist even if you have left it.

Perhaps, if you run it successfully in the next 50 years, you could turn it over to your grand kids! Perhaps you might develop other business interests in the future and move on, so you'd have to sell it to someone else.

There are business structures where the microbrewery is automatically dissolved if you leave, but there are those that allow the brewery to continue existing long after you have left.

Now that you understand the main things that you need to consider when selecting a business structure for your microbrewery, let's look at the main types of structures that you can pick from as well as their advantages and disadvantages.

The main business structures I will discuss include: a sole proprietorship, a limited liability company (LLC) and a corporation. Here is a detailed analysis of all three structures:

Sole proprietorship

If you set up your microbrewery as a sole proprietorship, there are certain advantages and disadvantages that will come with it. Let's first look at what this structure means before we delve into its pros and cons.

A sole proprietorship is the simplest type of business structure, and that makes it a favorite among small business owners such as mom and pop shops. When you run a sole proprietorship, you manage all aspects of the business, and you are personally responsible for all transactions that are related to the business.

From a taxation and a legal standpoint, you and your business are pretty much the same (you are not separate entities). You can own the business for as long as you want to, and you can sell it in the future or pass it along to your heirs (if you name the microbrewery after yourself, the new owner may need to change its name).

Since the business isn't a separate entity, it's you that has to pay tax on the income that you make from the business. However, you have to comply with the licensing laws of the federal, state and local governments as they relate to the taxation of breweries and microbreweries.

Taxation of microbreweries that are structured as sole proprietorships can vary in the degree of complexity depending on where you are. As I have mentioned, alcoholic products (in this case beer) may be subject to "sin tax" so they may be taxed at a higher rate than other products.

This means that as a sole proprietor of a business that sells such a product, you may have to pay a slightly higher tax rate, or you may pay a lot more for permits and licenses. If you choose to create a sole proprietorship, make sure you visit the Small Business Administration website to find out exactly what the law in your jurisdiction stipulates.

The main advantage of structuring your microbrewery as a proprietorship is that you get to have complete control over all the decisions that have to be made at the microbrewery. You don't have to consult with anyone when it comes to deciding which equipment to buy, which recipe to brew, or where to set up your operation.

That means that you get to go with your gut and you don't have to compromise anywhere, and as a result, you can explore your creativity a lot further when it comes to crafting your beers.

It's also very cheap and easy to set up a sole proprietorship. This means that you don't have to spend the bulk of your startup capital hiring lawyers and accountants, and you can, therefore, channel all your resources towards buying the best equipment for your microbrewery.

There is also not that much formality that is involved when creating a sole proprietorship. Many people go into micro-brewing because they are disenchanted with the formal nature of regular jobs, and if you have a strong desire to march to the beat of your own drum, a sole proprietorship can be a very appealing business structure for you.

In terms of tax implications, with a sole proprietorship, you don't have to pay the corporate tax rate, which means that even if there is a sin tax involved, you still may get to keep more of your money than someone who structures their microbrewery as a more complex business entity.

The last advantage of structuring your microbrewery as a sole proprietorship is that it's much easier to get out of the business should you choose to do so. If you wake up one day and decide that you want to pursue other interests, all you will have to do is sell off the business at your own discretion.

However, if it's more complex than that (especially if you have investors, debtors, and creditors), you may not be at liberty to unilaterally sell your microbrewery.

Now, let's look at the downside of structuring your microbrewery as a sole proprietorship. The first and perhaps the most significant disadvantage is the fact that sole proprietorships don't offer limited liability protections. That means that your personal assets are at risk of being auctioned off to settle debts and other expenses that are related to your microbrewery.

Like any other businesses, microbreweries aren't without risk. There are many things that can go wrong as you operate your microbrewery, so it's generally unwise to leave yourself exposed to liability.

For example, being a sort of mini-factory, your microbrewery has a lot of mechanical components that pose an inherent danger to the people who work for you—they could get injured on your premises, or they could develop certain medical conditions as a result of working for you for prolonged periods of time.

As for the product, since you are experimenting with different recipes, there is always a chance that you could come up with a bad batch that could give your drinkers stomach issues, and the more litigious ones could sue you as a result.

There is also the chance that you could buy some of your supplies on credit, and you would have to settle with your suppliers even if your sales decline and you end up with cash flow issues as a result.

If you choose to set up your microbrewery as a sole proprietorship, your own house, car, investments and personal savings will be used to settle all these kinds of liabilities.

For that reason alone, you shouldn't set up your business as a sole proprietorship.

Another reason to avoid using the sole proprietorship structure is that it makes it easy for you to confuse your personal finances and your business finances.

Unless you have separate accounts and records for your business, you won't have a proper picture of your profits or losses, and this could cause you to make bad decisions.

For example, if an expense arises at your microbrewery, you will have no qualms about taking money out of your personal account to cover that expense (and vice versa). It's wise to use a business structure that lays out a clear distinction between your business and your personal finances.

When you structure your microbrewery business as a sole proprietorship, it becomes extremely difficult for you to raise capital through normal channels.

Many private investors may be willing to give you cash in exchange for stock in your microbrewing business, but if it's a proprietorship, there is no stock to sell.

Also, when you are dealing with lenders such as banks, they are less likely to think of your business as credible if it's just a sole proprietorship.

Financial institutions tend to have caps on how much they lend to individuals, but they are more flexible when it comes to lending to full-fledged companies.

Limited Liability Company

A Limited Liability Company (LLC) is a great business structure for a microbrewery from day one. In many industries, people are advised to start off as sole proprietorships and then upgrade to LLCs when they post significant growth, but microbreweries are among the few kinds of businesses where it's more advisable to start as an LLC (at the very least) right off the bat.

When you start your microbrewery, there are just two things that you need to ensure your business structure does for you—the first is that your business structure should protect you from liability, and the second is that it should allow you to raise capital. The LLC is the simplest type of business structures that gives you those two benefits.

The main advantage of an LLC as I have mentioned is that it offers you limited liability protections, but that only works if you do everything by the book. When you set up your microbrewery as an LLC, you have to make sure that you do everything that is required of you under the law, such as record keeping, documenting meetings, and separating your personal and your business expenses.

Even if you structure your LLC in such a way that you are the only director, you still have to hold meetings (by yourself!) and write down all the minutes of that meeting; including the business decisions that you have made.

Remember that in as much as the LLC protects your personal assets from liability if you get sued, that protection could be taken away if you don't run your business in accordance to the rules of operating an LLC in your state. Make sure that you talk to a lawyer to understand exactly what you can or can't do should you choose to structure your microbrewery as an LLC.

The LLC structure also makes it fairly easy for you to get investment capital from banks, credit unions, or private investors. If you create an LLC and you come up with a sound business plan, you can pitch your idea to an investor and get him/her to either offer you a loan or to purchase stock in your business.

When you register your LLC, you will have to declare the nominal capital value of your company from the very beginning, so it's easy for you to sell certain percentages of your company in exchange for money to cover your startup costs.

For example, some microbrewers have been able to get the money they need by selling small percentages of their businesses to friends, family members, or "angel investors."

Also, as you register your business, you have to list the assets that are owned by the business, and you can then be able to borrow money against those assets—the LLC structure makes this quite easy to do.

One disadvantage of structuring your microbrewery as an LLC is that it costs more to do this than it would cost you had you chosen to set it up as a sole proprietorship.

However, many brewers have found that it is worth it to pay more to create an LLC given the simple fact that it offers limited liability protections.

Another disadvantage you may have to deal with if you set up your microbrewery as a single member LLC (where you are the only owner in the company) is that many states aren't particularly keen on honoring liability protections, and they may simply rule against you even if you have done everything right.

To avoid this, you may want to sell a small portion of your microbrewery to someone you trust, and make him/her a member of the board (just for the record).

Many people make their spouses, parents, or even kids part owners of their LLCs to ensure that they keep the liability protections.

Setting up your microbrewery as an LLC may allow you to find a way to compensate your employees when you have limited capital at the beginning.

You may have a difficult time hiring talented brewers at the start because you lack the money to compensate them adequately, but some of them (particularly those who believe in your vision) may be willing to forgo part of their salaries in exchange for stock.

Corporation

A corporation is a great way to structure a microbrewery if there are multiple owners and investors.

This means that if you are creating your business with several people with the intention of borrowing money from multiple investors, and hiring a number of employees (both owner and non-owner employees) a corporation may be the way to go.

As a business structure, a corporation is designed to accommodate a lot of complexity, so the more complex the ownership of your microbrewery is, the more the need for you to form a corporation.

One disadvantage of setting up your microbrewery as a corporation is that you could be subjected to double taxation. This comes about because you will have to pay tax both as a business and as an individual.

This means that when your microbrewery makes money, you will pay corporate tax, and then when you pay yourself as a stakeholder, you will again pay tax on that amount. There is a way to avoid double taxation.

You can elect to structure your business as an S-Corp. This will allow you to pay tax only as a stakeholder and not as a business (the explanation for how S-Corps work is a lot more complex than that, but all you need to know here is that they keep you from paying tax twice under certain conditions).

Another disadvantage of structuring your microbrewery as a corporation is that there is a lot of administrative work involved in the process, and you may even need to hire lawyers and accountants or put them on permanent retainer.

This means that you will have to pay a lot of money to set up and to run the corporation and that the administrative work can distract you from focusing on your core job function, which is to craft excellent beer for your customers.

There are conditions where it could be wise to structure your microbrewery as a corporation, but generally speaking, if you are starting your microbrewery as a single owner or you are partnering with a few friends, a corporation may be overkill in your case.

So, which structure is the best?

Of all the three structures that we have looked at, the LLC is the most reasonable structure for your microbrewery because it strikes the perfect middle ground when you weigh its merits and demerits in the context of a normal microbrewery business.

You don't want to overcomplicate things by setting up a corporation, but you also don't want to make things seem so informal by setting up a sole proprietorship—that just leaves the LLC as the perfect option as your business structure of choice.

Finally, where the business structure is concerned, you have to remember that you have to try to limit your liability as much as possible so it may be wise to put some of your assets under an entirely different entity in order to protect them further.

For example, if you have enough capital to purchase the building or the lot on which your microbrewery is located, you should make sure that you hold the land and other real estate assets under a different company than the one you are using to run your microbrewery.

Holding property under different companies may reduce the chances of you losing everything in case one of your companies is found liable on certain legal issues.

Chapter 3: Permits and Other Requirements You'll Need in Order to Get Started

Micro-brewing (and the brewing industry in general) is heavily regulated, and that means that there are lots of conditions that you have to meet before you can operate your business legally.

You should be prepared for the fact that you will need a lot more documents, permits, and licenses than you would in other industries because that's just the norm when you are dealing with a controlled substance such as alcohol.

In this chapter, let's take a look at all the "I"s you have to dot and the "T"s you have to cross before you can be allowed to open your brewery, no matter where you are in the country.

We have to mention that the requirements may differ from state to state or even from county to county, but the federal requirements are the same no matter where you are.

Getting your microbrewery name and beer names trademarked

As you register your microbrewery, and as you get started, one thing you have to do is to ensure that you trademark the name of your brewery to prevent other people from copying you (or trademarking it themselves).

A trademark is a word (or a combination of words), a phrase, a design, or a symbol which distinguishes your products from those of others.

The micro-brewing industry has become quite competitive lately, and that means that if you experience significant success, people might try to copy you in order to steal your customer base.

Trademarking your microbrewery name gives you a legal basis upon which you can take action to prevent other brewers from copying you.

In order to trademark your brewery name, you have to start by filing an application with the USPTO (the United States Patent and Trademark Office).

You may have a bit of a challenge if you try to trademark commonplace names, so it's better to come up with a name that you believe to be unique.

For example, if you come up with something such as "Jack's Beer," it's highly likely that you will find someone else has already trademarked it.

You need a name that is unique, creative, and one that captures the essence of your microbrewery.

When you file for a trademark with the USPTO, they will review your application and decide whether or not to grant you that trademark request.

Usually, if there is a problem with your trademark application (e.g., if your trademark request is in conflict with an existing trademark), the USPTO will respond with something called an "office action," and you will then have six months to address the issue that the office has raised.

If you don't respond within that window, they will automatically dismiss your trademark request.

If your trademark request doesn't seem to raise any red flags when you first file for it (or if you are able to resolve any conflict that arises within the stipulated timeframe) the USPTO will publish your trademark symbol so that the public can see it, and anyone who feels like your trademark will infringe on theirs can come out and raise their concerns.

If in 30 days (from the date of publication) no one objects to your trademark request, the USPTO will go ahead and register your trademark (in most cases, they will start the process 12 weeks after the publication date).

You have to understand that the trademarking process can be quite long (usually it takes 12 to 18 months from start to finish) so the best option for you is to initiate the process as early as possible and to start operating your business as you wait on the USPTO.

In many cases, you will eventually be able to get your trademark (even if you have to make a few modifications to the initial application).

It may be helpful to seek the counsel of a lawyer who specializes in intellectual property law because the trademark application process can be complicated and confusing, especially if you are navigating it for the first time.

You also need to remember to file trademarks for all your beers (those that you come up with at the beginning, and those that you create along the way). There is fierce competition in the micro-brewing business, and if you waste time in trademarking your beer, and it becomes popular, you may have to deal with unscrupulous brewers who might want to infringe on your brand.

Once you have come up with a logo and artwork for any beer that you have created, you have to initiate the trademarking process right away (even if you haven't yet managed to get the trademark for a particular design, the fact that you have already started the process gives you an upper hand, legally speaking).

You have to be careful about using a logo or particular artwork before you are sure that no one else has anything similar, because if it turns out that you are infringing on someone else's trademark, you could get sued.

Getting a "Brewer's Notice" from the TTB

The term "TTB" refers to the Alcohol and Tobacco Trade and Tax Bureau. It's the federal government agency that is responsible for collecting the Federal excise taxes for products such as alcohol, firearms, ammunition, and tobacco.

The agency also ensures that all business within the tobacco and alcohol industries comply with certain specific marketing guidelines for the purposes of consumer protection, and it regulates the way that all sorts of breweries can label or package their products.

It is responsible for issuing federal permits that allow commercial beer makers and tobacco companies to operate.

Getting the "Brewer's Notice" from the TTB is the most important step that you will take towards getting licensed to operate a microbrewery.

This is also one of the most difficult and time-consuming steps in the whole process of forming a microbrewery, so you have to make sure you get started on it as soon as possible.

So, who needs a license from the TTB? Well, pretty much every kind of brewer. If you plan to make beer for your own consumption (or to be shared with a member of your family), you don't need a TTB license.

However, anything more than that, whether it's as small as a Nano-brewery, or as large as an international beer company, has to be licensed by the TTB.

The TTB must approve the recipes that you use, the operations that you set up, and even the labels and packages that you use for your beer.

Before you can begin to make beer, you must first send a Brewer's Notice Application alongside with a Brewer's Bond to the agency, and the agency will then take steps to approve your beer.

In some cases, the TTB will come over to the site where you intend to set-up your brewery, and they will carry out an inspection to make sure that everything is in order before they can give you the Brewer's Notice.

The TTB is also concerned with the integrity of the people to whom it offers licenses to operate, so they may carry out a background check on you as the owner, as well as other directors in your company, members of your staff, and even minority shareholders (they have to make sure that you are not backed by illegitimate investors).

In the case of microbreweries, they also want to make sure that your company is not actually owned by a larger brewery (because that would be fraud).

The application process for getting a Brewer's Notice is fairly straightforward. Once you have registered a business that requires TTB regulation (in this case your microbrewery), you have to submit an application.

This can be done online on the ttb.gov website, or you can find the necessary forms, fill them, and send your application in by mail (the online application method is recommended because it's convenient for all parties involved).

The process may seem complicated if you aren't used to dealing with government websites, but there are lots of tutorials that the agency has created to help guide you as you fill in your application.

If you visit the ttb.gov website, you can find a list of the statutes and laws that you need to be familiar with if you want to be fully compliant with the agency's requirements.

You have to be extremely cautious when you are filling your application because you want to make sure that you avoid making even minor errors in the process. Some microbrewers have reported having their applications delayed for months just because they missed a single detail, or they put down the wrong information on certain boxes.

You must know how you intend to make your beer (this means that you need to have a detailed recipe of your beer) and you have to make sure you add that information to the application that you send to the TTB.

If your recipe seems vague, or if it doesn't meet standards that the TTB finds acceptable, they can deny you the Brewer's Notice, or ask you to make changes to your application.

You also need to list the kind of equipment that you intend to use in your brewing process, as well as the nature of the facilities where your microbrewery is going to be located.

For instance, you may have to specify the make and model of some of the systems and tanks that you will be using, because the TTB needs to know that your brewery is capable of producing beer under standard and sanitary conditions.

When you send out your Brewer's Notice Application, you also have to specify how you are going to label and market your products.

If you intend on making certain claims about your beer, the TTB wants to make sure that those claims aren't false, and that you don't mislead the consumer.

They also want to make sure that you don't inadvertently create packaging material or marketing slogans that make your beer attractive to kids (for example, you may come up with a cartoon for your logo only to find out that the logo is rejected because it appeals to underage kids).

Being a government agency, the TTB doesn't discriminate, so as long as you have all your ducks in a row, and as long as you adhere to all of the laws, they will approve your microbrewery.

Some entrepreneurs are nervous about putting huge amounts of capital into setting up a microbrewery before they get TTB approval, but that is rarely a problem.

Even if your initial application is rejected, the TTB will let you know what changes you need to make, so that your microbrewery can be compliant.

Like many other government entities, the TTB has to deal with issues such as being understaffed, and underfunded, so it's highly likely that your Brewer's Notice will take longer than you initially expected.

If you want your application to sail through smoothly, you have to do everything in your power to get things right the first time. Remember that even if there is no glitch, the process still takes 6 to 12 months, so ensure that you apply at your earliest convenience.

Getting requisite State and Local Government licenses

When you apply for your TTB license, you also have to apply for an Alcoholic Beverage Permit from your state (it is better when you do this simultaneously instead of waiting for one license to come in before you apply for the other because time is an important factor).

Applying for a state permit is going to be challenging for one main reason—the Alcoholic Beverage Permits are issued by different agencies and bodies in different states, so it's hard to tell which agency you are going to be dealing with, and what kind of procedures they have in place.

Still, you can check the Small Business Administration website in your area, or you can just run a simple online search to find out what agency is in charge of issuing Alcoholic Beverage Permits in your state, and then try to figure out the rest of the details from there.

Some states have "Alcohol and Tobacco Divisions," others have "Liquor Control Boards or Commissions," while others have "Food Safety Divisions" within their Departments of Agriculture.

There are lots of other different agencies responsible for issuing alcohol permits, but these days, no matter what state you are in, you should be able to fill out your application online, and the agency in question will definitely have content and other resources to help you do things correctly.

The state will require you to provide a number of documents (some states will readily issue permits with a minimal number of documents, but others will make you jump through hoops before they can issue you with a permit).

You have to make sure that you have all your documents in order especially when you are applying for a license from the state because state agencies tend to be less forgiving when you make certain mistakes.

They won't hesitate to hit you with fines for submitting applications with errors or to charge you high processing fees if they have to handle your documents for a second time.

Although there is a federal cap of 15 thousand barrels a year when it comes to the production capacity of a microbrewery, federal law doesn't specify the lower limit, for microbreweries, so some states have taken the liberty of coming up with their own guidelines (not just for the quantity of beer produced, but also for other aspects of microbreweries).

Make sure that you are aware of any and all requirements that are specific to your state.

In some states, you might be required to send your liquor license application in along with basic business documents, floor plans of the building where you have set up your brewery, your personal history form (so that they can do a background check), and even a Brewer's Bond. Some states require Brewer's Bonds while there are others that don't.

A Brewer's Bond is a lump sum of money that you have to give to a licensing body as a surety for the protection of the government, the public, and even your consumers. The TTB requires a Brewer's Bond, and so do some states because they want to make sure that you don't fail to pay tax as a producer of an alcoholic beverage.

If you fail to pay tax, the TTB or the state in question will use your brewer's bond to cover your tax obligation.

As it is right now, several states have been considering getting rid of the brewer's bond altogether because it increases the startup cost of legitimate businesses (some states have managed to remove it completely), but until this happens where you live, make sure that you consider it when you are calculating your startup costs.

Getting insurance for your microbrewery

Like any other beverage manufacturing business, you need to have comprehensive insurance coverage if you are to operate a microbrewery, so getting all your insurance documents in order is a key requirement before you can set up shop.

You also have to note that it's not just one kind of insurance that you will be getting; you might have to get different insurance policies to cover different scenarios, or if you are lucky, you might be able to negotiate a deal with your provider where some insurance policies are packaged together.

Let's look at the various types of insurance that you might need for your microbrewery.

First, you have to get General Insurance (the term General Insurance refers to many forms of insurance, mainly with the exception of life insurance). This will help you get compensated in case you encounter major financial events along the way as you operate your microbrewery.

You will also need to buy Health Insurance for yourself and your workers. Since running the microbrewery is your main job, you have to get insurance through the company.

That means you have to first add yourself to the payroll of the company (either as the CEO or the manager). The law requires you to offer Health Insurance to all your employees, so make sure that you are compliant.

Your employees will be more loyal and motivated if you provide them with a decent health insurance package, so don't just go for the package that meets the minimum legal requirements.

You also have to get Liquor Liability Insurance. It's easy to assume that if you are a microbrewery which doesn't serve alcohol on its premises, you may not need this kind of insurance.

However, that assumption is wrong. You may be surprised by how litigious people can be.

Someone could buy your product (whether on your premises or elsewhere), drink it, injure himself or others, and then sue you. Surprisingly, you may also be liable for the actions of your patrons if your microbrewery doubles as a brewpub.

Sometimes, even if legal claims seem to be frivolous, you may need to settle such suits just to avoid the bad publicity so it could be really helpful if you had good Liquor Liability Insurance.

A brewery is technically a factory, so as long as you employ workers, you need to have a robust Worker's Compensation Insurance policy. No matter how well organized your brewery is, there is always a risk that your workers could be injured on your premises, or that they could fall ill due to exposure to harmful substances.

Almost every state will require you to have this type of coverage so that your employees don't lose their wages when they fall ill or they get injured (this coverage also takes care of scenarios where employees die, and their families need to be compensated).

If you have commercial vehicles, you will need Commercial Auto Insurance. If you own the property on which your business is located, you will need Property Insurance.

You also need Overhead Expense Business Insurance. Finally, in case all of your insurance policies fail to cater for certain scenarios (or the claim exceeds what the company can payout) you will need Umbrella Insurance.

Some forms of insurance are legally mandated, but others are elective. As a business owner, you have to make sure that you look beyond what the law obligates you to do, and you have to make sure that you do everything possible to protect your microbrewery from both foreseeable and unforeseeable liabilities.

Comprehensive list of requirements

There are lots of other certifications, permits, and licenses that you might need to start your microbrewery (in some cases, you may need these things immediately after you have started your business).

I will not go into details discussing each of these items, but we will list as many of them as possible and offer a brief explanation of what they are so that you can use this segment as a sort of checklist when you start your own microbrewery.

Nevertheless, make sure that you consult with an attorney and other necessary professionals to ensure that your business is set up correctly. Most of these documentations are basic legal requirements, and you may need to obtain them from (or present them to) the federal, state, or local government. The requirements include:

- Business Liability Insurance: We have already talked about all the different types of insurance that you will need for your business.

- Health Inspection Certificate: Since you are producing a beverage that is going to be consumed by the public, you need certification to indicate that your premises are up to the legally mandated standards of cleanliness.

- Food and drinks handler certificate: you will need to acquire this certification as you start your microbrewery, and you have to provide some training for your employees in order to retain your certification.

- Taxpayer's ID: If you are running a sole proprietorship, you will use your individual tax ID, but if you have an LLC or a corporation, you will need to apply for a Taxpayer's ID for the business.

- Fire inspection certificate: The local fire department has to approve the fire safety compliance in your business premises.

- Business license: This is usually issued by the local government.

- A Certificate of Incorporation: Issued when you file documents to open the company.

- A Business Plan: It's possible to start a microbrewery without one, but that is not recommended. You will need it as a blueprint to help you run your business. It will also come in handy when you want to raise funds.

- Recent inspection report for your microbrewing facilities: You need this as proof that the building is structurally sound.

- A food and drinks manager identification card: This may be necessary for some jurisdictions, but not all.

- A liquor license.

- Trademark licenses: You need these both for your microbrewery and your beer brands.

- Standardized non-disclosure agreements (NDAs): You will need these because you want to keep your employees from disclosing your recipes and other trade secrets to rival brewers.

- Letters of offer/employment agreements.

- An employee handbook: You need to create one in order to let your employees know how to relate with each other in the workplace.

Chapter 4: Drafting up A Winning Business Plan

Just like any other business, the only way for your microbrewery to succeed in the long-run is by having a winning business plan from the very beginning.

For you to create a winning business plan, you have to be willing to dig deeper than everyone else to understand how the micro-brewing business works, and what can set you apart from the microbreweries with which you will be competing directly.

A microbrewery business plan has sections and chapters that are similar to those used in an ordinary business plan, but the content within is what makes the real difference—as they say, the devil is in the details.

The intention of this chapter is to help you understand the aspects of business planning that are of specific importance in the micro-brewing business, so instead of focusing too much on the generic steps of a business plan, we will try as much as possible to focus on those segments that are unique to this industry and crucial to your success.

A standard microbrewery business plan should at the very least have the following sections: An executive summary; a chapter on Market Analysis; a chapter on SWOT Analysis, a chapter on Financial Projections and a chapter that lays out a Marketing Plan.

Your microbrewery business plan would be incomplete (and therefore ineffective) if it doesn't provide answers to the following fundamental questions: What are your projected startup costs?

What are your projected monthly expenses? How will you find the perfect location for your business? What criteria will you use for hiring the best possible employees? What strategies are you going to use to find the right distributors?

Let's look at the various crucial segments of an effective microbrewery business plan.

The Executive Summary

This section is very crucial because it will determine how potential lenders and investors will think about your microbrewery business.

Like in any other business plan, the executive summary is supposed to be an overview of the entire plan, but the difference is in what you need to highlight.

A winning Executive Summary should start by discussing the location of your microbrewery, and explaining why that particular location is the optimal place for a business such as yours.

You should briefly mention whether you intend to purchase the property where you will set up the business, or whether your intention is to lease or rent it.

If you are to lease the place, mention the period of the lease in the executive summary—potential investors will be interested to know if your lease is secure because they are skeptical about investing if you can't guarantee that you can renew your lease in the long term.

The Executive Summary should talk about the product; in this case, the beers that you are planning on brewing. You should make sure that you mention the number of different beers you intend to make (at the beginning and also in the long run).

If there is something special about how you plan to brew your beer to make it distinguishable from other brands in the market, make sure you mention that too.

It may seem like a cliché, but it's important to add your Mission, and Vision Statements to the Executive Summary because potential investors want to understand your motivations and your long-term plans.

These statements also help anyone reading your business plan to understand why your microbrewery is different from the hundreds of other startups out there.

The Executive Summary should also contain a brief and clear breakdown of the structure of your microbrewery business.

Potential investors will want to know who makes up your company, and what roles everyone plays.

The management structure of a microbrewery doesn't have to be that complex—the important thing is that everyone in the business should have some sort of title, and a role that is clearly defined.

In most cases microbreweries will need the following essential personnel: A CEO (usually the owner of the microbrewery, and that's you in this case), technical and administrative staff (maybe engineers to maintain the equipment, chemists to monitor the quality of each batch, sales and marketing people to help you sell your beer, accountants for tax purposes, a lawyer, manual workers, and maybe a janitor).

The executive summary doesn't need to mention who you are going to hire.

Because you are still at the planning stage, the important thing is that you have to list all the roles that each person in the business structure is going to play.

The Executive Summary should mention how you intend to make a profit, and if necessary, it should give projection numbers so that the reader has a general understanding of what your potential is and what kind of investment you need.

The Executive Summary should end with a sort of call to action. If you need funding, mention towards the end of the Executive Summary that you are seeking investors.

You should also talk briefly about what kind of investment you want (whether you are selling stock or looking for a loan).

Finally, invite the readers to keep on reading the rest of the business plan by explaining that all of the questions and concerns that they may have will be addressed in detail within the main body of the document.

Market Analysis for Microbreweries

Lots of people who are writing their first business plan often confuse Market Analysis and Marketing Research. These two are entirely different things.

In market analysis, what you are trying to do is to prove to the investor (or anyone who reads your business plan) that there is an actual market out there for your product; that there are people out there who will be willing to pay money for your beer once you start producing it, and that there are good reasons why those people would buy your product and not someone else's.

In the case of microbreweries, market analysis involves looking at trends in the beer and the alcohol market within the geographical region where you intend to set up your brewery, identifying the segments of the population which will make up your target market, and articulating the qualities that will make your product more appealing to members of your target market.

Market Analysis can sometimes be referred to as Industry Analysis (although you shouldn't get too caught up in the industry at large because doing so can keep you from paying attention to your local market, which is what you should be doing as a brewer).

There is no getting around it. If you want to understand the market trends in the micro-brewing industry around the world, the country, and even your city, you have to do a lot of research.

Even if you don't need any funding from investors, you still ought to put in a lot of time and effort into figuring out market trends because that kind of knowledge is crucial to your success.

If you have been paying attention to news articles about beer consumption in the U.S or around most of the developed world, you have probably learned that craft brew consumption has increased steadily over the past decade or so, while the consumption of big brand beer has either slowed down or stagnated.

That kind of statistic can be the motivating factor that gets you to go into the micro-brewing business in the first place (and you have to summarize such stats in your business plan), but you should pay a lot more attention to the market within your immediate surrounding.

For example, if you want to set up your brewery at a certain location, start looking at beer consumption trends within a few miles of that location. That is not the kind of information that you will find in macroeconomic reports or even on online forums.

You may have to do the leg work. Visit other microbreweries in the area and find out how they are doing (it may help if you don't disclose upfront that you are going to be their direct competitor).

You should also visit the pubs in your area and talk to bartenders to find out if they buy beer from microbreweries in the area, whether the patrons in those pubs prefer craft beers over popular beer brands, and what kind of feedback customers are giving the bartenders.

If you have some money, it could be wise to hire a local Market Research firm to help you carry out surveys in pubs within your region. It's better to spend a bit of money doing market research than to sink vast sums of money on capital costs, only to find out later that the market is not as viable as you had assumed.

Once you understand the market trends, you should then go ahead and identify your target market. Remember microbreweries are sort of a niche businesses because their products appeal to a certain fraction of the population, and not to everyone.

Try to come up with a "buyer persona" for each of the beers that you will be producing. This means that you should create a sort of psychological profile of the kind of person for whom you are creating that beer.

Maybe your target market comprises of young professionals, college students, tourists who visit your town, etc. When you understand exactly who it is that is going to pay for your brew, it puts you in a much better position to make that perfect brew for him or her.

A crucial part of Market Analysis is understanding who your competitors are going to be. Generally, there are two kinds of competitors that you will have to deal with as the owner of a microbrewery: direct competitors, and indirect competitors.

Your direct competitors will be the other microbreweries, Nano-breweries, brewpubs, and even craft breweries that sell their products within the same geographic area as you.

Your indirect competitors will be the large breweries (even though they sell beer just like you, yours is a microbrewery, so you have to think of it sort of as a separate market), the distilleries that sell spirits in your area, and even the wineries.

Once you know who your microbrewery's direct and indirect competitors are, you should figure out what your competitive advantage is. A competitive advantage is something that gives you a certain edge in the market over both your direct and indirect competitors.

Try to imagine that you have set up your microbrewery across the street from another microbrewery: what do you have to offer, that the other guy can't?

It could be a secret ingredient, a special recipe, a proprietary brewing process, knowledgeable employees, a cost-cutting procurement plan, a prime location, or anything that you can capitalize in order to outsell your competitors.

The fact that there are so many microbreweries means that it can be difficult to find a competitive advantage, but if you dig deep and do a lot of research, you will definitely be able to identify a few competitive advantages.

Once you have all your market analysis data, you should present it in your business plan in as much detail as possible, and as objectively as you can. If you manipulate market analysis findings to exaggerate the viability of your microbrewery, it will come back to haunt you later on when things are up and running.

SWOT Analysis

This is a tool that is used to gauge the viability of any business venture, and many people in the business world have come to expect it to be part of your business plan, so you should make sure that it's included.

SWOT stands for Strengths, Weaknesses, Opportunities, and Threats. It's one of the easiest analytical tools to use even if you have no business training whatsoever.

If you are unable to do the SWOT analysis on your own, you can always hire a consultant with business experience to come, study the microbrewery business that you are trying to start, and do the analysis with you.

When analyzing your strengths, you have to think about all of the good things about your microbrewery business, and you have to list them down in as much detail as possible. If you have an experienced team, a great location, a wonderful recipe, etc. you have to include them on your list of strengths.

Analyzing weaknesses is much more difficult than it seems, but with some objective introspection, you can find lots of weaknesses in your business. Remember that identifying a weakness means that you are aware of it, so you are more likely to manage it should it cause problems once you have opened your brewery for business.

Your weakness could be that you have limited starting capital, that you have to start on a very small scale, or that your ability to expand is limited by the amount of space you have on your business premises.

We are often blind to our own weaknesses so it would help if you asked people around you to give you an honest assessment of your microbrewery business in order to see if they can identify any weaknesses that you may have overlooked.

Opportunities are external conditions that you can use to your advantage in order to improve your business and increase profitability. The fact that more people are drinking craft beer and that the number is bound to increase over the next few years is an opportunity that you can exploit.

New technologies such as social media marketing can also be thought of as opportunities. These are examples of opportunities that apply to the whole industry, but there are bound to be some other opportunities that are particular to your microbrewery, so try to identify and document as many of them as possible.

Threats are external conditions that are potentially detrimental to your business. Common threats include things like changing regulatory and tax policies at various levels of government and the fact that lots of people are venturing into micro-brewing which could an increase of competition and limit your market share.

Again, you need to get good at identifying the threats that are very specific to your situation.

As a point of caution, you should remember that SWOT analysis is just meant to help you and your investors understand what you are up against so that you can plan better. If you have lots of weaknesses and threats, it doesn't mean that your business isn't viable.

It just means that you need to come up with sound strategies to mitigate against them. Similarly, if you have lots of strengths and opportunities, it doesn't mean that success is guaranteed, it means you have to maximize the utility of each of those positive factors, so you have to come up with a plan to do that.

To create a winning business plan, you should break down all the points from your SWOT analysis and explain how you are going to take advantage of the positive factors and diminish the impacts of the negative factors.

Financial Projections

From a business standpoint, the section on Financial Projections is the most important part of your business plan because it contains all the figures that investors will need in order to decide whether or not to fund you.

Even if you have the money to start your microbrewery on your own, you will need this section to understand how much money you need to get started, what it's going to cost you to keep things running, and how much profits or losses you are likely to make.

The first thing you have to do in this section is to report your startup and capitalization costs. When you hear someone quoting a round number to an investor (e.g., saying that he needs a quarter million dollars to start a business), that number is usually arrived upon after adding the costs of individual items that need to be purchased, labor costs, and operating costs for the first few months.

In your business plan, don't just pull numbers out of thin air. Make sure you do your due diligence, and you calculate the costs of everything that you are going to need.

First, you should compile a list of all the items that you'll need, figure out how many items of each kind you'll need, and then find out what it costs to buy every item from an authorized distributor.

In as much as you want to keep your startup costs to a minimum, you shouldn't always go for the cheapest items—go for the items that are made by a reputable manufacturer. For the more expensive systems, make sure that you get a warranty.

Always round up your price estimates and factor in the effect of inflation on your prices (for instance, if you make your cost estimates right now and you get your funding six months down the line, the cost of certain items could have risen slightly, and you will be unable to buy them if you didn't give yourself some wiggle room when you were coming up with your estimates).

If you have to import certain equipment, you have to make sure that you consider the tariffs in place as well as the cost of shipping the equipment to your location.

Some people calculate their startup costs based on the price of second-hand brewing equipment, and that's okay if you have connections with people who can find such equipment for you, but you have to understand that the maintenance cost of second-hand equipment is usually a lot higher, so make sure you consider that before you choose to go in that direction.

Apart from the cost of equipment, you also have to consider how much it would take you to set things up and to acquire all the legal documents and permits that you need before you can start producing beer.

Make sure that you add; the cost of registering your business; the cost of hiring consultants, lawyers and accountants to help you with the registration process; the cost of remodeling your business premises before you can set up your microbrewery; the cost of rent for at least one full year; the cost of at least one month of inventory; the cost of getting comprehensive insurance coverage; the cost of office equipment (furniture, computers, printers etc.); miscellaneous costs; and many others.

One mistake that many entrepreneurs make is that they assume that they'll be great money managers, and they limit the overhead costs in their initial estimates, only to find out later that some expenses are inevitable.

In terms of labor costs, you need to have enough money to pay your employees for the first three months before you even open your microbrewery. You also need enough cash to pay all your utility bills over the same period of time.

As part of your financial projection, you also need to be able to come up with estimates of your sales, and your profits or losses for the foreseeable future. You can make your projections based on the records of other microbreweries in the area, or you can base your projection of other market research data that you would have gathered during market analysis.

Even though there are standardized methods used to make fairly accurate projections, the truth is that entrepreneurs are given a lot of freedom to come up with their own projections for various reasons. One reason is that investors like entrepreneurs who are optimistic.

Another reason is, profit projections also work as targets. This means that if you tell an investor that you will make a certain amount of money in the next five years, that investor may fund you based on that promise in the hope that you will work as hard as possible to live up to it.

When you are making projections on the profitability of your microbrewery (whether they are long-term or short-term projections), you should try to come up with numbers that are as conservative as possible.

If you exaggerate your potential for profitability, one of 2 things might happen; either the investor refuses to fund you because your plan seems too good to be true, or you get the funding, and you spend the next few years trying to accomplish a goal that is unrealistic.

Other things to address

In your business plan, you should also explain where the location of your microbrewery is going to be, and why that is the optimal location for your business. You need a location that is within or close to a busy area, where there is a lot of foot traffic.

This is especially important for the brewpub part of your business (if you have one) because a big percentage of your customers are going to be the ones who chance upon your establishment. A prime location is key because, without it, many people may just never find out about your microbrewery.

Another location factor is the size of the building where you will be setting up your business, and the kind of flexibility it will offer you in case you want to provide other services that complement your microbrewery.

For example, if you want to have a gift shop (where you sell t-shirts and other merchandise or paraphernalia), you need to find a location that has enough space to enable you to do that.

If you want your microbrewery to have a tasting room or even a restaurant on the premises, you have to make sure that when you do your location scouting, you narrow down to potential locations that are big enough for those add-ons.

Include pictures of your chosen location in the business plan to get your potential investors to see the value in having a microbrewery at that particular location.

You should also include an explanation of how you are going to find the right distributors. You need to come up with a comprehensive plan on how you are going to reach out to restaurants and bars in your target area, and how you are going to convince them to carry your beer and to serve it to their customers.

You have to explain in your business plan whether you intend to bottle your beer at the beginning or in the future because the distribution strategies for kegs and for bottled beers are different. With bottles, you can visit grocery stores and liquor stores in your area and try to convince them to put your beer on their shelves.

In some states, there may be laws preventing you from distributing your own beer, so if you live in such a place, you have to explain in your business plan how you are going to identify reliable distributors who have the required distribution license, and how you intend to partner with them to move your product.

However, in most other states, there are self-distribution prohibitions so you may have to come up with a plan that involves buying or leasing vans or trucks to distribute your beer to restaurants, bars, and other establishments.

The last major section in your business plan is about ideas and strategies that will help you market your brand and maximize sales. In this section, you will outline both online and offline marketing strategies that you intend to use, and you also have to assess the viability of each aspect of your strategy.

We will be discussing practical marketing strategies in a later chapter in this book, but for now, it's worth mentioning that the more well-thought-out your plan is, the more likely it is to succeed.

Chapter 5: Different Equipment You'll Need

There are many factors that you need to consider before you decide on what kind of brewing equipment you will need for your microbrewery.

At this point, you would have drafted a well thought out business plan, so you will have some idea of how much beer you want to produce, how much money you are willing to put into your venture, and at what rate you wish to scale your business in the coming months or years, so you will have to make sure that your brewing equipment fits within those constraints.

You need to have clear production requirements in mind before you decide what size or number of tanks you will need for your brewery. If your establishment doubles as a bar, you have to think about the number of patrons that you will be serving.

The equipment you purchase should have the capacity to produce the volume of beer you want, and you should be able to calibrate it to produce the kind of beer you want (for example, some microbreweries are focusing on making beer with a high alcohol content, but some older models of brewing equipment aren't designed to produce this kind of craft beer).

You will also factor in your sales projections before you select your brewing equipment. You have to understand that when you get started, it may take you a while to craft a beer that actually sells, so you can't sink all your capital into high capacity brewing equipment with the assumption that you are going to generate a profit from day one.

Depending on your budget, you can opt for brand new brewing equipment, or you can buy used equipment from a microbrewery that has shut down. In some areas where microbreweries are common businesses, you might find companies that offer rental brewing equipment which microbrewers can hire on a particular time schedule.

While this model may work for some microbreweries, we don't recommend it because if you want long-term success, you need to have your own means of production. It may be okay to use rental equipment if you are still testing your beer recipes before you become fully invested.

Speaking of beer recipes, they are some of the most important considerations that you need to keep in mind when you are deciding what kind of brewing equipment you need to buy. How many different recipes do you intend to brew?

If you intend to make just one or two recipes, it might be okay to invest in one or two sets of high-capacity micro-brewing equipment. However, if you plan on experimenting with many different recipes, you might want to invest in multiple sets of medium or low volume brewery equipment. All of this will depend on the business model that you have decided upon.

Before you decide on the kind of equipment you need to buy, you must also understand how the brewing process works. If you know a thing or two about making beer, you understand that it is a batch process and that each batch of beer can take about a month to make.

Since you are dealing with micro-brewing, each batch should take between 2 to 4 weeks on average.

The first time-intensive process is the fermentation process, and this should take about one week. The next one is the conditioning process, which could take between one and three weeks.

After you have fermented and conditioned your beer, you will put it through the actual brewing process, which should take maybe six to eight hours.

The length of each step in the process varies depending on the kind of beer you are making, but irrespective of what process you are using, or how much time it is going to take you, at the very least, you have to invest in the following equipment: fermentation systems, cooling systems, filter systems, mash systems, a controlling board for electronics and pumps, cleaning equipment, and kegging or bottling equipment.

Let's take a look at each of the main types of equipment to understand why you need it, how it works, and how to select the right kind.

Fermentation systems

A fermentation system or a fermenter is a vessel that is used to hold the beer wort during the fermentation process, which, as we have mentioned, takes about a week or so.

There are many different designs for fermentation systems; some systems come with components such as cooling attachments, insulation, pressure gauges, inlet and outlet valves, covers, temperature probe gauges, and wheels for mobility.

A perfect fermentation system should have most of these components, but it is okay to buy a system that lacks some of them, and then buy those missing components separately.

Alternatively, you could also figure out how to use your fermentation system without those components. Remember to always go for the more cost-effective alternative.

Fermentation systems, particularly those meant to be used in microbreweries, are made from different kinds of materials. There are fermentation systems that are made of glass, plastic, stainless steel, concrete, carbon steel, or even wood. Nowadays, most standard fermentation systems are made of stainless steel, but you have to factor in your personal preferences.

If you are setting up your brewery in such a way that patrons can observe the brewing process as they enjoy your end product, it may be worth it to invest in a glass fermentation system for display purposes.

Plastic fermentation systems are cheap, and they are meant for brewers on the lower end of the market, but there are issues with durability, and cleaning, so they may not be the best choice if you want to make a capital investment.

Most plastic materials tend to have micro-pores, and particles of your beer wort could get stuck in there even if you clean the vessel, and those particles could affect the quality of your subsequent batches.

Wooden fermentation systems can give your brewery a vintage feel, but they are costly, hard to maintain, and quite difficult to integrate into an automated brewing process.

Stainless steel fermentation systems are most commonly used in the micro-brewing industry, and it's for a good reason—they are fairly priced, durable, and easy to clean and maintain.

The best fermentation systems are those that are conical in shape (most of them will be cylindrical at the top with an inverted cone at the bottom). Ideally, a good fermentation system should be a conical shaped stainless-steel system.

This type of fermenter has a valve at the bottom, which allows you to manage the trub in the batch that you are fermenting. The term 'trub' refers to the debris made of hop and other material that settles to the bottom of the fermentation tank.

When you are using a cone-shaped tank, the trub will easily settle at the bottom. The conical shape makes it extremely easy for you to remove the trub from the beer solution as it ferments.

In the beer making process, there is primary fermentation, and then there is secondary fermentation.

The primary fermentation process is done with the trub in the beer solution, while the secondary process is done without the trub.

If you have a high-quality conical stainless-steel fermentation system, you will be able to use the value at the bottom to get rid of the trub after the primary fermentation process.

You may, therefore, be able to use the same tank for both primary and secondary fermentation.

That means that if you invest in this kind of tank, you can save yourself from having to buy the fermentation tanks in pairs, or having to pay for the labor cost that is involved in manually removing the 'trub' from the beer solution and then putting it back into the fermentation tank.

Another great advantage of using conical stainless-steel fermentation systems is that when you remove the trub, you can collect it, wash it and reuse the yeast that you collect in the process.

This can significantly cut your costs in the long run. By definition, microbreweries are focused on quality more than quantity, and in an attempt to produce high-quality beer, many of them buy and use special kinds of yeast, which can be very expensive.

If your fermentation system allows you to reuse your yeast, then purchasing new yeast won't be a running cost that could affect your profit margins.

Also, when you invest in a high-quality stainless-steel conical fermentation system, you would be able to make clear beer, which many in the micro-brewing industry tend to think of as the "holy grail" of craft beers.

The conical fermenter separates a lot of the sediment from the wort, dumping it at the bottom of the tank, and if your intention is to make clear beer, you could accomplish that by removing as much of the sediments as possible.

Cooling systems

Breweries need properly sized and robust cooling systems, because cooling is required at various stages of the beer making process. You need a cooling system that can regulate the temperature in various tanks in your microbrewery, and make sure that your beer remains at the optimal temperature for the necessary biochemical reactions to occur.

Most microbreweries use cooling and glycol systems that have the ability to perform more than one cooling function at the same time. The cooling system (often referred to as the chiller) is arguably the most important part of your brewery, and it's going to be more costly than most of your other equipment.

While other systems are used in just one stage of the brewing process, the cooling system is used on numerous stages, either directly or indirectly.

Even in the brewing stages where the cooling system isn't integrated into the process (such as milling, mashing, 'lautering' or boiling), the fact is that heat is generated during these processes, and you will need a cooling system to remove that extra heat from the batch after you are done with each of these processes.

One of the main uses of the cooling system is to cool down the wort after boiling and before fermentation as we have mentioned.

There are different types of cooling systems that perform this function in a number of different ways, so you will select one for your microbrewery depending on how much capital you are willing to invest, how much space you have to spare for the installation of your cooling system, the operating costs you are willing to shoulder, and how precise you want your cooling system to be.

Let's look at the various steps in the beer making process where cooling is required, and how the cooling system is used to get the job done at each of the stages.

One of the more common cooling systems for the wort on the pre-fermentation stage is called the Cold Liquor Tank (in micro-brewing circles, this tank is simply called the CLT).

This is usually a stainless-steel tank that is designed with an external heat exchanger, or with cooling jackets. Between brewing cycles, this tank is filled with water which is then chilled to 35 degrees Fahrenheit. This water is then pumped to the wort exchanger (here the ratio of the wort to the pumped water is usually 1 to 1).

The wort, which has just been boiled, is then cooled to the right fermentation temperature. In modern breweries (which are designed to conserve energy), the chilled water which has just been used to cool the wort, and is now a bit hot, is directed to the hot liquor tank, where it is used for preparing the next beer batch.

The CLT tank is a part of the cooling system, and when you are selecting one for your microbrewery, you have to make sure that it is big enough to contain enough chilled water to ensure that the brewery can run for the next 24 hours.

This means that in order to decide what size of CLT tank to purchase, you have to multiply the capacity of your brewery by the number of times you brew each day to find the optimal capacity of your CLT tank.

The second type of cooling system works in 2 stages. The first stage is similar to the one we have described above when talking about the CLT; where chilled water is used to remove as much heat as possible from the wort, using a heat exchanger.

In the second stage, glycol is used to remove the remaining heat from the wort, until it gets down to the fermentation temperature.

In some cases, the water from the city supply has to be cooled before it enters the heat exchanger because, in some cities, the water is supplied at a significantly higher temperature during certain seasons.

If you have to chill the water before it enters the heat exchanger, you may have to use a different type of heat exchanger, such as one that is sealed (the problem with this is that such heat exchangers are hard to clean).

There is a more complex wort cooling method which requires three stages to remove the excess heat from the wort.

While this method works extremely well and is highly effective at bringing the wort down to the required temperature, the problem is that you need a lot of extra equipment, and that means that it's more expensive to acquire, set up and operate.

You also need the cooling system to regulate the temperature during the fermentation process. The fermentation process is naturally exothermic, so the more the wort ferments, the more the temperature rises.

If you don't take action to regulate the temperature at the fermentation tank, the fermentation process will be inhibited.

You have to understand how much heat will be produced from each fermentation tank before you can figure out the capacity of the chiller that you need to use at this stage.

Glycol chillers are the most efficient cooling systems that you can use at this stage of the brewing process.

When the fermentation process is done, you have to crash-cool the beer batch to make sure that you lower the temperature down to what brewers refer to as the "holding temperature."

This temperature varies depending on the type of beer you are making and the size of the fermentation tanks that you are using, but as long as you have a standard cooling system, it should do just fine in this stage.

After the holding stage, the beer is transferred to the conditioning tank. Cooling is required at the conditioning stage, but the cooling load is quite small compared to that of the other stages in the process.

After conditioning, the beer can then be packaged. The packaging process also requires cooling. If you have the capital, you can integrate heat exchange plates into your bottling or canning line to make sure that the beer is packaged at the optimal temperature.

Alternatively, you can chill down the whole room where the packaging occurs.

You have to remember that even though most of your cooling system is designed to be out of the way, and much of it is automated, you still have to make sure that it is well maintained so that it functions optimally.

Make sure that you read reviews from other brewers before you pick a cooling system because it is one of the most important capital investments you are going to make as a brewer.

Filter systems

In tiny breweries (such as Nano-breweries or home breweries), you can get away with just using sheet filters or lenticular filters for your beer before you package or serve it.

However, if you are running a microbrewery or a much larger type of brewery, you are going to need to invest in a more complex filtration system if you want your beer to be stable for a long time, and if you want to accomplish this using a cost-effective method.

There are generally four main stages that are involved in the beer filtration and clarification process. These stages include primary, trap, fine, and final membrane filtration.

Each of the four stages of filtration performs a very specific function. The primary filtration stage is meant to remove bulk yeast and other solids from the beer.

The trap filtration stage gets rid of additives that were added to the wort but have now performed their functions. The fine filtration stage is meant to further reduce the levels of yeast in the beer, as well as the finer particles which managed to pass the first two stages.

The final membrane filtration stage involves the removal of microorganisms from the beer. The microorganisms include bacteria and yeast, which if left in the beer, will lower its shelf-life considerably.

In the primary clarification stage, you can either invest in DE or cross-flow filters. The DE filtration system uses a form of screen that is coated with a coarse filter aid. You will be able to use the DE to clarify the beer until the filter cake accumulates to a certain predetermined depth.

If you use a cross-flow filtration system at the primary clarification stage, you have to understand that this process usually requires a centrifuge to remove yeast and other bulky particles.

You may not need to add a filter aid during this process, but you have to remember that the system you use has to be powerful enough to remove most of the larger particles to avoid the damage of the latter components in your entire filtration system.

A cross-flow filtration system is a great option for your microbrewery if you care about your carbon footprint and water usage because it is a lot more efficient than the other method.

Trap filtration is also called particle filtration, and it is used in breweries to make sure that you get a bright filtrate without the use of filter aids. Depth filters are often used to remove the particles at this stage.

Depth filters work well when you are dealing with particles of different sizes. Depth filters have components known as depth cartridges, modules, and sheets, all of which make use of a dense matrix of filaments (usually, its organic materials such as glass or polymers).

The depth filter traps particles on the surface as well as throughout the depth of the column.

In the 'fine' or 'final' filtration stage, there is an extremely fine membrane that removes bacteria and yeast.

The membrane used here can be easily damaged, so it's crucial to ensure that the filtration in the prior stages is thoroughly done so that you don't end up with big particles on the final filtration stage.

In some systems, the final filtration stage is combined with the trap filtration stage in one system.

Filtration is also used in a process known as beer recovery. This is where breweries harvest yeast from the fermented wort so that they can use it in future batches instead of wasting money buying new yeast every time.

There are several types of filtration technologies that can be used in this process. These technologies include the use of a filter press, the use of centrifuges and decanters, and the use of crossflow technologies.

The filter press method is no longer recommended because of sanitation concerns, but you can pick one of the other two methods, depending on personal preference or budget.

Another important filtration process in the brewery world is known as utility filtration. Here, the term utility refers to things like water, air, steam, and gases that you are going to use in the beer making process.

You have to understand that the slightest concentration of particulate matter or chemicals in your "utilities" can have a significant impact on the taste or the quality of your beer.

Many municipalities and cities provide water that is okay for human consumption, but if you are making a craft beer, you have to make sure that you filter your water for two main reasons.

First, you don't want your water to add unwanted tastes to your beer. Second, you don't want the water to destroy your brewing equipment in the long run (e.g., by causing rust or corrosion).

There are many different filtration systems that you can use to filter your water before you use it for brewing. There are sediment filtration systems, carbon filtration systems, water disinfection systems, and reverse osmosis filters.

Before deciding on the kind of filtration system you want to use, you can take a sample of water from your main supply and have it tested in a water quality lab. From there, you can then figure out what needs to be done to improve the quality of that water.

The gases you use at your brewery include carbon dioxide, oxygen, and nitrogen. Some of these gases may have dust and oil, so you have to make sure you get rid of that.

In most breweries, fine cartridge filters are used to remove particulates from the gas. There are two ways to install gas filters: you can install them at a central place, or you can install them at various points of use.

Mash systems

To understand what mash systems are, you first have to understand what the mashing process is. Mashing refers to the first stage of the entire brewing process, where the crushed grains are mixed with water to form a thick slurry which brewers refer to as "mash."

The mashing process makes it possible for the malt (germinated barley) and any other cereal that you may be using to be chemically broken into sugars and proteins. These sugars and proteins dissolve in the mash water, and that is how the wort if formed.

Some breweries have their own malting houses, while others buy malt from suppliers. When the malt is brought in, it is milled together with some additives to form a mixture which brewers call "grist."

When we talk about the mash systems, we are referring to the equipment that is used to mill the malt as well as the equipment where the actual mashing occurs. After it is milled, the grist is mixed with hot or warm water in a ratio that is carefully controlled.

The mashing system includes a grain handling system and a mash tun. Depending on the size of your brewery and your budget, you can select a grain handling system that uses a bucket conveyor, a trough conveyor, a flex auger, a tubular chain conveyor, or a pneumatic system.

The bucket conveyor and the trough conveyor are mostly used in larger breweries where the ratio of the grains used to the water added doesn't have to be too precise.

The flex auger system and the tubular system are often used in microbreweries, and they are fairly affordable options compared to the pneumatic system.

The pneumatic system is a bit costly but is it very accurate when it comes to measuring the amount of grain that has to be delivered at any given time.

The pneumatic system is also very flexible because it can carry the grain vertically and through 90-degree bends, so you don't need to use a lot of space to set it up.

If you have the capital, we recommend using the pneumatic grain handling system in your microbrewery. If your budget can't allow it, it's okay to use the other systems, or even to transfer the grain manually.

The pneumatic system will start at the bottom of your grist tank and carry the grain all the way to the top of your mash tun. Before the grist enters the mash tun, you have to preheat the mash tun.

Usually, this is done by running hot water through the mash tun and draining it off. After that, you have to add "foundation water" into the mash tun before you add the grist.

The mash tun has a "hydrating pipe," which serves as the inlet that brings in the water, as well as a chute that brings in the grain.

When investing in a mash tun, make sure you buy one that has as many programmable functions as possible. This is because you want to avoid a situation where you have to hire people to man the processes that are involved at the tun. You should not skimp on the mash tun.

You should buy the highest quality tun that you can find for your microbrewery because there are many complex mechanical and chemical processes that go on at the tun, and if you have a poor quality one, it could break down after just a short period of use.

Controlling board for electronics and pumps

In modern breweries, most of the processes are fully automated and programmable. You have to invest in control systems for the various processes in your brewery.

There are many advantages to having a high-end control system. For starters, you can reduce your labor costs because you won't have to hire people to carry out particular processes manually.

Secondly, you can save a lot of time and speed up your brewing processes when things are fully automated. Most importantly, the control system allows you to focus on perfecting the formula of the brew and producing your beer rather than wasting time doing manual labor.

When choosing control systems for your brewery, it's wise to go with the newest and most technologically advanced controls that you can afford. You also want a centralized control system, and one that covers as many processes as possible, starting from grain handling all the way to the treatment and disposal of wastewater.

When you have a PLC (programmable logic control) unit, you will be in a better position to see to it that you put out a product whose quality is consistent because all you have to do to replicate a nice batch of beer is to input the same commands under the same conditions.

As you automate things, it's up to you do decide how much control you still want to retain over the brewing process. Many microbrewers succeed because they create a beer that has a personal touch to it, and the danger with automating everything is that you might lose that personal touch.

In as much as you want to make your brewing process as efficient as possible, don't go for a system that completely eliminates the manual functions. Instead, set up your system in such a way that you can switch between manual and automatic options whenever you need to.

Here are some additional things that you should consider when selecting a control system for your brewery: make sure that it uses a PLC to create a simple user interface (if the operator interface isn't simplified, you would have to rely too much on your engineering staff, and you may not be able to operate it on your own); it should have digital displays for parameters such as temperature, pump speed, etc.; it should have unlimited customization options.

Cleaning equipment

All brewing equipment needs to be cleaned; some equipment has to be cleaned after every batch, while other equipment has to be cleaned after a regular interval of usage. After one batch of beer is made, there will always be some residue on the equipment, and while this residue may not necessarily ruin the next batch, you want to avoid letting it stay in there for too long.

There are two main methods of cleaning brewery equipment. The first method is the manual method, and the second method is the CIP (clean in place) method.

Manual cleaning involves workers using handheld equipment to clean and to sanitize the tanks and other equipment at the brewery. Usually, you and your employees will just use brushes, pads, pieces of clothes, and water hoses to scrub and wash down the brewing equipment.

Many microbrewers use this method because equipment that is designed to be manually cleaned is fairly cheaper than the equipment that has to be cleaned in place.

One thing you have to remember when using the manual cleaning method is to make sure that you allocate specific functions to all your cleaning tools and equipment to prevent cross-contamination.

For example, if you use the same equipment to clean the fermenting tank and the tanks you use to store the beer after brewing, you could contaminate the storage tank with yeast.

If you can afford to, you should invest in CIP systems. These systems were first pioneered in the dairy industry, and they were quickly adopted in other beverage industries.

The main advantage of these cleaning systems is that they reduce the amount of labor and the time that that is required to complete the cleaning process. CIP systems are designed to recirculate the water and other chemicals that are being used in the cleaning process, so in the end, the systems reduce the usage of water and cleaning agents by about half.

Because there is minimal human involvement in the CIP process, the chances of being exposed to harmful cleaning agents or other biochemical solutions at the brewery are very low, and this minimizes the health risk to your employees. CIP systems are also more thorough because unlike manual cleaning, there is no chance of human error in these processes.

In CIP systems, there are spray devices that are used to deliver the cleaning fluids to the surfaces and the equipment that has to be cleaned. Spray devices can either be static (those that stay in one place) or dynamic (those that move around).

CIP systems can also be classified into two different categories: single-use and recovery type. In single-use CIP, the cleaning fluids are discharged after use, while in recovery CIP, the fluids are recovered at the end of the cleaning cycle, so they can be reused later on.

If you are not able to afford a CIP system when you first start your brewery, you should come up with a plan to invest in one in as soon as possible (preferably the recovery-type CIP) because it can end up saving you a lot in terms of time and labor costs.

Kegging or bottling equipment

Most microbreweries start off by packaging their beer in kegs, and they only start bottling after they have had some success selling their beer to local pubs.

So, you want to invest in kegging equipment during phase one of your plan, and if you are successful with some of your brands, you can then purchase bottling equipment.

It's recommended that when you start a microbrewery, you should have your own outlets (whether right at the brewery or at other locations) because unless you have a ready market for your product, it's easy to go bust.

Kegging your beer helps you deliver it to your customers without incurring too high of a cost.

To be able to keg your beer, you need a Bright Beer Tank (commonly referred to as a BBT). These tanks are used to store beer after it has been filtered, and they can also be used to keg the beer.

They are designed to be hygienic, and they can be pressurized with carbon dioxide. In larger breweries, kegs can be filled in the upside-down position using precise equipment, but most microbrewers fill their kegs directly from the bright tank while monitoring the pressure all around to make sure that the beer is well carbonated, properly preserved, and that it is filled to the correct level.

Your bright tank should have a pressure gauge, and it should be connected to a clean source of pressurized carbon dioxide. The tank should then be connected to a manifold system at the bottom, which should, in turn, be connected to the empty kegs using sanitary hoses.

As long as you have the skill necessary to keg your beer, you wouldn't need any more equipment than what has already mentioned.

If you decide to bottle your beer, you have to understand that the production volume of a microbrewery is fairly low, so you don't need to invest in an elaborate automated bottling assembly line. You can just use a bottling line that is manually operated.

Even if you only have a handful of floor workers, you may still be able to bottle hundreds or even thousands of beers per day. If you go into bottling, you should really be more concerned with labeling and branding.

Some microbrewers choose to order bottle labels in bulk from printing firms and then apply them using either hand-operated or electrical label applicators. Label applicators are fairly affordable, and you can always get a great bargain if you order labels from a printing company and stockpile them so that you can use them on several batches.

These days, microbrewers have the option of printing and labeling their beer bottles using one continuous setup right at the brewery floor, so they don't have to order labels from a third party.

If you choose to use this method, you have to invest in a high-quality label printer, and you also have to purchase a label applicator that is compatible with the printer that you have (the best approach is to buy them from the same supplier to make sure that there are no compatibility issues).

After that, you will only have to buy rolls of labels whenever you want to bottle a new batch of beer.

Chapter 6: How to Raise Capital for Your New Business Venture

Securing funding for your micro-brewing business is perhaps the biggest hurdle that you will have to overcome on the journey to starting your business. If you are well off, and you are capable of fully funding your microbrewery venture, then you are in the super-minority.

Most people who start microbreweries are young (mostly male) entrepreneurs who don't have much in terms of savings.

Even if you have savings and you want to transition into micro-brewing after retiring, it's unwise to sink all of your life savings into the business, so unless you are completely comfortable with it, you should look for other ways to get funding.

In this chapter, we will discuss the most viable funding methods out there today, we will look at the merits and demerits of each method, and we will leave it to you to select the one that works best given your particular circumstances.

So, here are the methods one can use to find the necessary funds for a microbrewery.

Bringing on investors

Bringing on investors is probably the most common way that most microbreweries get funding these days. In most cases, you would have to give up a small ownership percentage in your microbrewery in exchange for money which you can then use to cover your startup and early operational costs.

To successfully bring on investors, you have to be good at presenting your business in a positive light because you will be competing against a lot of other microbreweries or even startups in different industries.

There is an art to winning over investors. You need to start by preparing a comprehensive investor packet, which should contain all the information that prospective investors may need in order to make that crucial decision of whether or not to fund you.

Most savvy investors (including venture capitalists, banks, and even well-off acquaintances) expect entrepreneurs to be well prepared, and few of them would even consider giving you money if you don't have a full investor packet.

Your investor packet should have a business plan (a brief plan with all the crucial details should suffice), financial projections (your projections should seem well sourced and reasonable), and market analysis reports.

As part of your investor packet, you should provide a private placement memorandum because there are lots of investors who like to move fast.

Also, should you manage to convince someone to invest, you shouldn't waste time closing the deal because you don't want to give them a lot of time to reconsider.

Your investor packet is supposed to entice people and convince them to give you large sums of money, so make sure that it is extremely attractive.

If you have already come up with some design ideas for your microbrewery, make sure to use your logo and color scheme on the investor packet, and pay an experienced graphics designer to make your packet look fancy.

You have already heard that if you want to convince someone of something, you should show it to them instead of merely telling them about it.

This is where you have the upper hand as a brewer. Don't just tell investors that you have a great beer recipe, give them the opportunity to taste your beer!

You need to host a pitch party for your prospective investors. If you have already come up with a few recipes, and if you can get access to some brewing equipment, you should brew a batch of your beer and invite all potential investors to your pitch party, preferably on a date that is convenient for most of them.

At the party, they should all get the chance to at least taste some of your best recipes, and you should explain to them what's so special about your beer.

Pitch parties are usually effective when it comes to convincing investors who are on the fence about your product. If all goes well, by the end of the party, a few investors should be willing to give you cash.

In preparation for the party, you should make sure that you brainstorm and figure out what kind of questions investors may want to ask you, and you should prepare to show everyone that you are well versed with all the technical aspects of the beer brewing process.

If you are unable to supply satisfactory answers to potential investors at the pitch party, they may question your expertise or your commitment, and they may choose not to fund you.

Remember that with investors, their main interest is getting a return on their investment, so in as much as you want to show them the technical aspects of your micro-brewing business during your pitch party, you have to be able to address their financial concerns, such as: what criteria was used to arrive at the valuation that you have indicated in your investor packet, clear explanations for what you will be doing with their money, when exactly they will see some return on their investment, and the finer details about how you are going to structure your deal with them.

Some investors may not be able to make it to your pitch party, so if they can't come to you, go to them. You could schedule an appointment with potential investors, and when you go to the meetings, you could bring the investor packet as well as a sample of your beer (in a well-presented package of course).

Don't be afraid to bring bottles of your beer to pitch meetings, they are the perfect prop to help you close the deal.

Now that you understand how you can court investors, let's look at the advantages and disadvantages of bringing them in to fund your business. The main advantage of bringing in investors is the fact that they are giving you much-needed capital.

With so many competing startup microbreweries out there, you should consider yourself lucky if you find people or entities that believe in your idea, and are willing and ready to cover your startup costs.

Experienced investors are usually very particular about who they give their money to, so the fact that they are funding you should serve to boost your confidence in your venture. They are giving you access to financial resources without which your business wouldn't be able to exist.

Another advantage of bringing in investors is that they can contribute valuable ideas that can help your micro-brewing business succeed. Many investors tend to be seasoned entrepreneurs who know what it's like to start one's own business.

Some of them are usually professionals within the business and finance sectors, so they know a few things about business management. When they come in, they can provide you with a lot of valuable insights, and your business can benefit from their experience.

Since they are invested in your microbrewery and they are keen on getting a return out of that investment, you can be certain that the advice they are giving you is well-thought-out and that they have good intentions.

If you have multiple investors, it widens your network in business circles, and that increases your chances of getting distributors, customers, or even skilled workers.

The problem, however, is that investors come with their own set of challenges, and some of them can turn into big disadvantages for your micro-brewing business. For starters, when you take money from an investor, you have to give them equity, and that means that they now own a fraction of your company.

Depending on the terms of the deal you make with them, that entitles them to some rights. If you agree to give them board seats in your microbrewery, they may have a say on all major decisions in the future.

With some investors, you may be able to negotiate a revenue-based financing deal, so that they are entitled to a percentage of the profits that your microbrewery will make in the future, but you still retain ownership over your entire business.

Another problem with investors is that they may have their own vision for your microbrewery, and that would put you in conflict with them.

Investors offer you money and connections, but some of them have a tendency of wanting to control the way you do things so they may pressure you to make certain decisions that you don't want to.

Investors want a return on investment, and some tend to get impatient.

For example, if you sell 10% of your microbrewery to an investor in exchange for $100,000, and after you are up and running, a big brewery comes along and offers you $2 million for your entire business, the investor may pressure you to sell your company because he stands to double his money on that sell, and that's all he cares about.

When investors have the right to vote on major decisions about your brewery, they gain a lot of power over you, and in the end, it can feel like they are your bosses. Since you got into microbrewing partly because you like the autonomy, that feeling can disappear, and your job will start feeling like a regular 9 to 5.

Investors are profit driven, and sometimes, that can curtail your creativity as a brewer. They could push you to compromise the quality of your brew to increase production and to reduce costs, and that could cause you to lose your identity as an artisan brewer.

For these reasons, some microbrewers are skeptical about working with investors, and they are finding other ways to finance their microbrewery startups. If you too have concerns about ceding significant control of your business to investors, then you should consider one or more of the alternative funding methods that we will discuss in the rest of this chapter.

Raising capital via crowdfunding

There are plenty of crowdfunding platforms out there, and with that comes a funding opportunity for all sorts of entrepreneurs, including microbrewers. In fact, there are crowdfunding platforms that strictly raise money for businesses in the beer-making industry. Whatever crowdfunding platform you choose to use, your strategy is to get potential contributors to engage with your microbrewery by telling a great branding story, and making people feel like they are part of something unique.

You first have to decide what crowdfunding option you want to pursue so that you can create a campaign that works for the method of crowdfunding that you have chosen. There are generally four different crowdfunding models, and under normal circumstances, you have to pick one model and stick to it.

The first crowdfunding model is the donation-based model. Under this model, you will be seeking to raise money for your microbrewery by asking a very large number of donors to give you small contributions towards your project.

For example, if you need $50,000 in seed money, you will be asking hundreds of thousands of people to donate a dollar or more, in the hope that you would get enough donations to meet your target.

The donation-based model has its advantages and disadvantages. One positive factor is that you don't need much in terms of expenses to get started.

In fact, the upfront costs of creating such a campaign are pretty low. All you need to do is start a page on a crowdfunding platform, find ways to market it online and watch the donations start streaming in.

Another crucial advantage here is that the donors don't expect you to offer them anything in return for their donations, which means that if you succeed in raising money this way, you will be able to retain complete control over your microbrewery (you won't have to give away equity).

Another advantage of this crowdfunding model is that it also doubles as a marketing tool because it makes people aware of your beer brands and your microbrewery so that once things are up and running, you will already have a customer base.

The main problem with the donation-based model of crowdfunding is that it works best for campaigns that seek to raise fairly small amounts of money. Unless you have a serious marketing strategy for your crowdfunding campaign, the chances of failing to meet your funding targets are pretty high.

The second crowdfunding model is the reward-based model. Here, people will contribute fairly small amounts of money, and in return, you will reward them with certain prizes.

Since you are raising funds for a microbrewery, you could promise to send your contributors some beer, or you could offer coupons that allow them to get free drinks at your microbrewery once it opens (this works better if your microbrewery doubles as a brewpub).

The reward-based crowdfunding model is a good one for microbrewery startups because you don't have to put up any form of collateral in order to get the funding.

You can also raise money without the crowdfunding platform running a credit check on you, and contributors aren't too concerned with your track record or whether you have experience in the business.

You also don't need to hire lawyers or accountants to help you figure out how to create this kind of crowdfunding campaign. Most importantly, you don't have to offer equity to your contributors, so you get to run your microbrewery however you want to.

The main disadvantage of the reward-based crowdfunding model is that if you don't meet your funding target, you have to forfeit all the money that you have raised in the form of pledges.

For example, if you set your campaign target at $50,000, and you manage to raise $45,000, you won't be able to collect your money. This can be a painful experience for any entrepreneur, more so if you have been working hard to promote your funding campaign in your social circles.

The third type of crowdfunding model is the lending-based model. Here, you raise money from well-off strangers on various internet platforms, but it's all in the form of a loan that you have to pay back with interest.

When setting up the crowdfunding page on such platforms, you have to specify how much money you want, and what repayment timeline you are comfortable with.

Like the other two models we have discussed, the advantage with the lending-based one is that you won't have to give away equity in your company. You also have control over the amount of interest you that you pay (because you can set the loan terms).

If you find people who are okay with the interest rate you have offered, you could get very favorable loan terms. Also, your chances of getting funded are a lot higher because the people giving you money see it as an investment that will earn them interest.

The disadvantage of the lending-based crowdfunding alternative is that it can't double as a marketing tool because your funding page won't be seen by enough people.

Contributors may also be interested in finding out more about your credit history and your business acumen, but that shouldn't be a problem if you have all your ducks in a row.

The final crowdfunding model is the equity-based model. This is somewhat similar to finding investors because you will have to put up some equity in exchange for cash.

In this system, large groups of investors are able to fund your microbrewery startup, and each of them will get a fraction of the equity that you will put up when you create your funding campaign.

The equity-based crowdfunding model is good because you can get large sums of money from it (unlike the other models where it's difficult to raise lots of cash). You also don't have to put up your assets as collateral because as part owners of your microbrewery, the contributors will share in the risk.

Also, you will be put in contact with the investors (most of whom are experienced entrepreneurs), and they can offer a lot of useful advice, especially if you are relatively inexperienced on business matters.

The main disadvantage of the equity-based model is that you will give up some equity, so you no longer have complete control over your microbrewery. The other disadvantage is that the process is quite complex, and it will take a lot of time for you to receive your money.

This is because you are literally transferring equity to investors over the internet, and that means there are lots of legal and accounting processes that have to be followed.

While you can technically use any of the crowdfunding models I have discussed to raise cash for your microbrewery, you have to remember that no matter what model you choose, you need to have a very good strategy in order to appeal to potential donors, contributors, lenders, or investors.

The vast majority of crowdfunding campaigns fail, so you can't just do the bare minimum and expect people to throw cash at you. Make sure that you spend a lot of time creating online buzz for your crowdfunding campaign in the weeks and days before you launch it.

You can hire some influencers to promote your brand on social media, and if you are setting things up in a small town, you could do a press release and try to get some media coverage.

The crowdfunding arena is overcrowded with people looking for the exact same thing that you are, so you must do everything possible to stand out from the crowd and to get people to take notice of your campaign.

Founder loans

A founder loan is a loan that you give to your business with the expectation of recouping it once the business has taken off. In the context of a microbrewery business, if you have personal savings and you are okay with using them to fund your startup, you could give that money to your company as a loan with a clearly defined repayment plan.

If you have enough money to fund your microbrewery, you should be very careful in the approach you take to do this. Don't make the mistake of putting up a large sum of your money as nominal capital when you are incorporating your microbrewery business.

If you put up all your savings as nominal capital, all that money will now belong to the company (which is a separate legal entity), and you will have a difficult time recouping it if the business doesn't succeed. Instead, use a low amount of money as nominal capital as you deal with company registration, and when you are ready to make capital purchases, you should then give your microbrewery a founder loan.

There are lots of legal advantages to using a founder loan. If the business fails and it goes bankrupt, your loan will be given the same level of priority as that from any other lender, which means you won't lose everything. However, this only works if you make sure that your loan terms are clear, and that you service the loan according to those terms.

From a business standpoint, founder loans can help you win over investors because they show that you believe in your microbrewery idea and that you are willing to put your money where your mouth is.

For example, if you need to raise $200,000 for your microbrewery, and you give your business a founder loan of $40,000, investors will see that you are willing to bet your savings on the business, and this will increase their confidence in you and make them give you the rest of the funds that you need.

You could also use a founder loan to start at a very small scale, and once you get going, you can then leverage the brand you have created to expand your microbrewery and to increase production. For example, if you only have the cash to rent a small space and to buy one set of brewing equipment, don't be afraid to do that.

Investors and lenders are usually more willing to give their money to businesses that are already operational, and they are usually hesitant to fund businesses that only exist on paper, so if you can use a founder loan to get things started, that could increase your chances of successfully getting funded.

Deferred wages

This option doesn't necessarily fund your microbrewery business, but it can significantly reduce the startup cost, thus allowing you to get things off the ground with a lot less money.

The way it works is that you strike up deals with your employees, suppliers, and distributors, and anyone else you have to pay money to, so that instead of paying them immediately, at least in the first few months, you can pay them a small fraction of what you owe them, and then pay the rest later on.

This could work for you if you have built trust, if you are open and honest from the beginning, and if you have covered yourself from a legal standpoint.

There are lots of startups these days that make use of deferred wages and stock options to reduce their startup costs, so, if you can't get enough funding any other way, you could try this as a last resort.

As the CEO of your own microbrewery, you can pay yourself as much or as little as you want (as long as it is a reasonable salary), so there shouldn't be much of a problem when it comes to deferring your own wages. However, where your employees are concerned, there are a few things that you must take into consideration.

First, you have to know that you cannot blindside your employees or force them to take deferred payments. This means that you should let them know at the moment you are hiring them that you will have to do this.

Otherwise, you run the risk of violating employment laws. Second, you have to understand that deferred wages have negative tax implications for your employees, so you have to make sure that they aren't victimized.

Instead of deferring salaries by delaying them, you should strike an agreement with your employees to reduce their salaries at the present moment and then increase them in the future.

This way, for tax reasons, it looks like they got a raise, so they don't owe back taxes. You can only do this if you have written consent from each and every one of your employees.

To sweeten the deal for your employees, you could also offer them bonus incentives (these too should be done in writing so that the employees are confident that they'll be paid).

Incentive bonuses should be structured in such a way that they are contingent on certain future events. For example, you could create a bonus incentive that states that you would pay your workers once you have sold a certain number of beer barrels.

If you agree to pay the bonus at a certain time in the future based on the assumption that you would have made enough money by then, you will be in a lot of legal trouble if that time comes and you are unable to meet your obligation.

It's safe to assume that your microbrewery would probably never offer an IPO, but that doesn't mean that you can't offer stock options to your employees.

Owners of microbreweries have been able to hire talented people at reduced salaries just by offering them equity. In fact, instead of offering them vested stock options, you can give your employees percentages of the microbrewery right off the bat.

This gives them a sense of ownership, and it makes them more dedicated and more invested in seeing the company succeed.

Asset finance

Asset finance has been the refuge of entrepreneurs for such a long time that it's the go-to method of financing for a lot of startups that require massive capital investment in the beginning.

Asset finance is lending that's backed by business assets. For example, you could use your brewing equipment as assets to secure a loan from a bank, and as you start making money from sales, you could pay off that loan, and when you are done, you will be the full owner of the equipment.

One common asset finance option is hire-purchase. In this instance, if you need equipment worth $100,000, you would need to come up with the deposit amount (it could be as low as 10%) and you would then be able to buy the equipment with the agreement that you would have to pay the rest of the amount within a specific period, and with a certain interest rate.

You could either get the financing from the seller, or from a financial institution (say a bank or a credit union). In some cases, you may be able to negotiate a deal where you would defer the repayments for a while.

The advantage of using the hire-purchase method is that it greatly reduces your startup cost, and if you make timely payments, you end up owning the assets in question. The downside of hire purchase is that if your microbrewery doesn't start making profits as fast as possible, you could miss your payments, and your equipment could be auctioned off.

Another asset finance alternative is leasing. Here, you will be able to rent the brewing equipment from a company that provides such services, and you would make monthly payments.

The advantage here is that the equipment isn't yours, so when it depreciates, you are not losing any value. The flipside of that is that you are making periodic payments for assets that don't belong to you.

Leasing can help you get things started, but it's recommended that you should avoid doing it in the long run. Once you have made enough money, and you have decided that you want to stick with the micro-brewing business in the long haul, you are better off buying your own equipment.

Short-term credit

There are many forms of short-term credit that you can consider getting if you are starting a microbrewery. Short-term credit refers to situations where you can get cash, raw material, or other things that you need for your brewery with the agreement that you would pay in full in the near future.

You should only consider short-term credit if you are out of options because if you over-leverage yourself and something unforeseen happens, you could go bankrupt.

The first form of short-term credit is trade credit. In your case, you could get supplies (such as malt), or your brewing equipment from a seller with the agreement that you would pay for it after a short time.

You would then use the supplies or equipment to make your beer and sell it as fast as possible, and use the money to pay your creditor (businesses do this sort of thing all the time).

Another form of short-term credit is when you borrow money from friends and family with the agreement to pay them as soon as you start making a profit. This method is not recommended because if you are unable to pay, it will end up ruining your relationships.

Banks are also able to give you short term credit if you need it, but they always require some form of leverage. Be careful with this option because banks won't hesitate to claim your assets if you default on a short-term loan.

Chapter 7: How to Avoid the Embarrassing Problem of Not Having Any Customers

Figuring out how to find customers is going to be one of the biggest puzzles that you will have to ponder once you have started your microbrewery. The best approach to take is to start considering the customer in every decision that you make, and this should start long before you even set up shop.

You should make sure that when you come up with your beer recipes, you create a product that offers real value, and every time you brew a batch, you make sure that the initial value is maintained on a consistent basis.

You also have to identify your target customer as early as possible, and you need to create a product that you are absolutely certain will appeal to that customer from the very beginning. Marketing campaigns are meant to inform people about your product. They can't magically turn a bad product into a good one.

Another thing you have to keep in mind before you start marketing to customers is that you need to make your beer readily available to them in the first place so that when they encounter your marketing material or content, there is no confusion about what they need to do to get access to your beer.

You also have to remember that the marketing strategies that you select ought to be cost-effective. There is no use investing in a marketing strategy that causes you to lose money in the long-run.

You also have to make sure that no matter what communication channels you select for marketing purposes, you will communicate effectively, and you will do it frequently. You can't pass a message across just once and expect people to remember it forever.

You also have to keep in mind that when you market your beer, whether you do it online or offline, you have to deliver on each and every promise that you make.

Now that the basics are out of the way, let's look at how you can get customers by marketing both offline (in your local area) and online.

Marketing to businesses in your local area

Look around you. There are beer drinkers everywhere. Every adult you see is a potential customer.

Surveys have consistently shown that the vast majority of people aged 18 and above are at least casual drinkers (even though the legal drinking age is 21). What these surveys have shown is that there is a large cohort of drinkers out there, and even though they may prefer different types of alcohol (many may like regular beer, wine, or spirits), the bottom line is that they are willing to spend money on alcohol.

If your microbrewery is missing customers, you don't need to look far to find some. That guy walking past your front door is a potential customer.

You should target the people that live and work near your microbrewery, and that means that you have to do everything in your power to make them aware of your product and to convince them that it's of the quality that they want.

In any local market, growth is about who you know, so you want to make sure that you know (or are known by) as many people as possible, including business owners, employees of those businesses, members of the local community, etc.

To accomplish this, you need to get involved. You need to be an active member of the community so that they accept your business as an integral part of their lives.

The first thing you need to do is use fliers. Even before your doors are open for business, print out high-quality fliers and walk into every business in your local area, talk to the proprietors of those businesses, and ask them to hang your fliers on their notice boards.

Don't be afraid of doing the same thing with big offices. In fact, the more squared away the people seem to be, the bigger their need to unwind in the evening, so those "stuffy" office workers are probably going to be your best customers.

You should, however, be careful to avoid inadvertently marketing your beer to children (for example, if you want teachers at your local school to be your customers, you can't put up a beer flier on a school notice board).

There are all sorts of offers that you can create, depending on your marketing budget. If you don't have a brewpub at your microbrewery (or even if you just want to expand to other bars), you could offer your kegs to bar owners at a considerable discount, and this would incentivize them to put your product front and center at their bars, making it more visible to their customers.

If you partner with bar owners or bartenders, they could even help you with your marketing campaign and collect valuable feedback from customers on your behalf.

Generosity is important if you want to endear yourself to the community around you and to turn its members into your customers. Generosity here is more than just giving away a few free beers when you open the microbrewery or are offering the occasional discount during holidays.

Generosity means putting substantial resources into community projects and programs.

Any business can benefit from being perceived as "a pillar of the community," but as the owner of a microbrewery, you have to understand that getting that reputation is an uphill task for your business.

This is because many communities (even the more liberal ones) think of drinking as a vice, and as a beer marker, they may have a difficult time embracing you. So, you have to go above and beyond to make them like you.

You may not be able to sponsor the little league soccer team (because, again, you can't advertise to kids), but you can contribute to the community by taking part in social events, volunteering to help the less fortunate in the community, donating money towards projects and programs the community cares about, hosting your own community events, and taking up causes that help the community.

You can be able to convert a few locals into customers just by putting up a couple of park benches around town.

If there is a local armature sports league (say a softball league for small businesses and public entities in your area, you should rally your employees, form a team of your own, and sign up. It doesn't matter if you suck at it.

The important thing is that you are participating in a recreational activity with other businesses in the area, and that will help you make a lot of friends and loyal customers.

You should also give a discount to local organizations. This will not only endear you to the locals, but it will also make your beer brand more visible, and increase your customer base.

For example, you could put out the word that members of the fire department or employees of the accounting firm across the street can get their drinks at half price in your brewpub (or select bars that have your beer on tap).

The fact that you are giving a discount doesn't mean that you will be making a loss. Even if all you are doing is breaking even at the moment, you have to consider "customer lifetime value."

There is a reason why the coffee shops that give "law enforcement discounts" always seem to thrive. Discounts create customer loyalty, and that loyalty is more valuable to you in the long run than making a few bucks at that one moment.

When marketing to locals, you should find out about any local events or parties that are taking place, get in touch with the organizers of those parties, and offer them a deal to supply beer for the event at a discount.

For example, if there is a law firm in town that is having a Christmas party, they are definitely going to need beer in bulk, and therein lies the opportunity for you.

If you succeed in convincing them to let you supply the beer, many people at the party will get to enjoy your microbrew for the first time, and if it's any good, you will definitely win over a few long-term customers.

In order to know in advance about parties that are being organized in your local area, you should make friends with local catering businesses. B2B (business to business) connections are very important, especially if the two businesses offer services that are complimentary.

In this case, caterers can bring food, and you can bring beer, everyone can enjoy the party. If you strike up a deal with a catering business, they will be able to recommend your beer to some of their clients, and every now and then, you might get to supply beer to different events and parties, and the local community will start recognizing your brand a lot more.

The micro-brewing industry is known for its tradeshows, so if you want to market yourself locally, you need to participate in any tradeshows that breweries in your area are organizing.

You have to understand that if you want to sell your beer, you don't just market to the end consumer, you also market to industry players such as bars, and distributors.

When you hear that there is a brewing tradeshow anywhere within your target area, get in contact with the organizers of the tradeshow and get a booth as early as possible. Even if you are unable to secure a booth, you should go to the tradeshow anyway, because you never know who you are going to meet there.

When you get leads such as bar owners and beer distributors, whether it's at the trade show or anywhere else, make sure that you follow up with them.

Given the fact that yours is a new brand and that distributors and bar owners already carry a lot of beer brands, many won't be willing to commit to distributing or serving your beer outright, but even then you should make them a pitch and give them your contact information.

You never know when an opportunity may arise in the future. A bar owner could have an open tap, or a distributor could have an increase in demand, so make sure yours is the first brand that pops into their minds when such opportunities arise.

When marketing your craft beer offline, you have to understand that location matters. You should choose the location of your microbrewery with its marketing potential in mind.

For example, you should make sure that first and foremost, you choose a place that is densely populated.

You want to go for a location with a high population of young urban millennials because they are more likely to want to experiment with new beer brands.

Finally, where offline marketing is concerned, you have to understand that word of mouth is your greatest weapon, so make sure that you offer your customers a unique and enjoyable experience, whether they are drinking at your brewpub, or at any other bar that carries your beer.

You want to make sure that when your customers drink your beer, they feel the urge to go out and tell their family and friends about it.

This means that there is no getting around it— you just have to make sure that you create a great product, one that stands out from the rest.

If you don't have a great beer to begin with, then it doesn't matter how much marketing you do. You may deploy the most sophisticated marketing campaign yet, but drinkers will only turn into customers when you offer them a high-quality beer.

Online marketing

Today, online marketing should be a mandatory part of your marketing strategy, no matter what kind of business you are in. That's because people spend more time finding things online these days than they do in the real world.

If you are creating a marketing plan for your microbrewery, a big part of that plan should include strategies on how to increase your visibility on the internet, and particularly on social media platforms. Even if your target market is within a limited geographical area, there are ways to micro-target them over the internet.

You will need to have a website for your microbrewery, because people who become aware of your brand may want to find out more information about it, and a business website is the best repository for all the information about your brand.

You cannot rely on social media pages alone to do that job for you. These days, anyone can create a website or a blog using simplified online tools, so you don't need a lot of technical skills to do it.

You also have to learn to create content, including articles, images, and videos. It's easy to learn how to do all these things—the real challenge is to find the time and motivation to do it on a regular basis. If you can afford to, you should hire someone to be in charge of your online and social media presence.

As you create your brand online, one important thing you will need is a compelling brand story. Consumers these days, especially millennials and younger generations, don't just care about the product—they care about the story behind the product.

For you as the owner of a microbrewery, this means that you have to come up with a narrative that makes your brand seem interesting to potential customers. Your brand story could be the origin story of your microbrewery. Why did you start the microbrewery?

What makes your microbrewery better than every other similar business out there? You have to create a brand story that is unique, and one that your online audience can engage with.

Don't go with a generic brand story. Every other microbrewery out there is telling the same story—how the founder hated his day job, so he woke up one day, quit the job, and founded the brewery.

A story like that one is overplayed, and if you use it, it won't make you stand out in any way. You need to dig deep to come up with something that is heartfelt, something that evokes empathy, and something that makes your audience root for you.

In other words, you need a story that gives your brand a likable personality. It is okay to use classic storytelling tropes (such as the story of a hero's journey, or one of triumph over adversity) but your angle must be unique if you want to appeal to potential customers on social media and on the internet.

After you have your compelling brand story, the other thing is to invest in a brand design that is memorable. You have to understand that in the online world, people "judge the book by its cover" so make sure that your beer brand is something that people are attracted to or fascinated by.

People are going to look at the logo of your microbrewery, and the color scheme on your website and social media pages, and they are going to make judgments based on that.

Even if you are just getting started and you are only packaging beer in kegs before you expand to bottles or cans, you have to make sure that you invest in a great design, and you come up with a killer logo that will stand out from all the rest.

You should seriously consider starting a blog for your microbrewery. As I have already mentioned in this book, brewing is something that plenty of people are passionate about, and you are likely to get a sizable following if you write about it on a regular basis.

It's very likely that the people who order craft beers in the pub are also the kind of people who are interested in the beer making process, so if you run a blog where you share your experience as a microbrewery owner, you could get a considerable amount of readers, some of whom could end up becoming customers.

If you run a micro-brewing blog and you provide information that people find fascinating, you will be able to establish yourself as an authority on the subject, and people will, therefore, start trusting your skills as a brewer and they may want to taste your product as a result.

If you post quality blogs on a consistent basis, you will rank highly on search engines for terms related to micro-brewing in your area, and people will be able to find you online organically.

For example, when people type in your city and micro-brewing into search engines, the search algorithms will bring up your website among the first results if they detect that you have a lot of content on your blog that suits the parameters of the search term.

One thing you have to do is make sure that your blog posts are optimized for search engines. There is a lot of content online about search engine optimization (SEO), so even if you are new to the blogging arena, you shouldn't find it too difficult to learn how to do it.

Even though you can buy ads to get your microbrewery to show up when people search for related terms within your area, you should consider the fact that blogging is free, and if you do it well, you won't have to pay anyone to get good search engine rankings.

Blogging can connect people to your brand and make you seem more authoritative on technical matters and make you more relatable. As we have mentioned, you need to have a good brand story to win people over.

You should make sure that your brand story is well captured in your blog, and you have to keep referring back to it in order to reinforce it in the minds of your long-term readers and to introduce it to your newer readers.

The people who read your blog will want to go on a journey with you. If you start your blog in the months or weeks leading up to the launch of your microbrewery, they will root for you to successfully start your business, and they'll want to stick with you throughout every milestone.

These are going to be your most loyal customers, so don't miss out on finding them by failing to create a blog. It may seem hard to start a blog at first, but with time, writing it will come naturally.

That's because you will be handling a topic that you are passionate about, and you will just be recalling your personal experiences.

When it comes to social media marketing, you have to remember that there are very many angles to it and that your goal is to maximize visibility. The advantage you have here is that microbreweries are entities that are inherently social in nature—hanging out with friends and trying out new beer brands is probably one of the most social things that one can do.

You need to have a heavy social media presence, so for starters, make sure that you create a social media page for your microbrewery in any or all of the social media platforms out there. It doesn't matter what platform it is, or who it's targeted at: if a platform exists, you should be on it.

You should come up with a custom hashtag that is unique to your microbrewery, and you should use it across all platforms.

When you have a custom hashtag, and you use it consistently in many of your social media posts, you tend to create a conversation around that hashtag, and that tends to build brand awareness.

Your custom hashtag could be a condensed version of your microbrewery's name, or it could be the name of your most popular beer brand. No matter what it is, just make sure that it is short and catchy.

In social media marketing, you have to make sure that you are more inclined towards visual content. In as much as text content is crucial to the success of your social media campaign, the human brain is wired to respond to visual content such as pictures, gifs, and short videos, so make use of them to promote your beer brand.

Encourage your customers and fans to take pictures of themselves enjoying your beer and to post those pictures on social media platforms. People enjoy all sorts of seemingly silly challenges online, and you will be surprised to find a lot of people are actually sharing such posts.

For your social media strategy to work, you have to stay engaged with your customers and fans. When people make certain comments about your microbrewery, or they ask some questions on social media, don't just disregard them.

Engage them in a conversation, and make sure that there is some back and forth between you and them. This way, they will know that yours is the kind of business that values their feedback, and they are in turn more likely to become regular consumers of your beer.

Engaging with fans online shows that you are a microbrewer who cares about the patrons, so they'll feel the need to reciprocate by buying your beer.

You should also work with social media influencers to promote your beer brand. An influencer can be anyone with a large following on social media, so you don't necessarily have to go for those major social media stars.

Besides, you are looking for local influencers and not national ones, so they shouldn't be too hard to find or too expensive to hire. If there is a local social media personality with a few thousand followers, you can pay him or her to promote your beer on his or her pages.

You can get several of these influencers to do a few campaigns for you for a reasonable amount of money. They can post photos of themselves drinking your beer.

They can post videos of themselves touring your microbrewery. They can post messages recommending your beer. Influencers are very effective in convincing the people that already admire them for taking certain actions, so in most cases, you could experience an immediate bump in sales after an influencer recommends your beer.

Although you can hire social media personalities to promote your microbrewery, you might want to turn yourself into a popular personality as well, because you are your own best ambassador. In order to create a social media following of your own, you should put out as much engaging content as possible, and you should try to at least create a viral video about your microbrewery.

Don't do anything drastic or dangerous (a lot of people injure themselves or others trying to go viral). The easiest way to go viral is to participate in one of those viral challenges.

You just have to make sure that your brand is prominently featured in the video that you create, so that in as much as viewers will watch your video to see you perform some sort of stunt, they will get curious about your brand, and they may look it up online.

In the long-term, you want to build a fanatical social media following. You will be able to do this by creating a lot of social media content that is properly optimized for the platform on which it's to be used, and you have to organize a lot of promotions and events, to get more people to follow you. It's all about creating content that people find interesting.

In general, you want to build a robust online community across multiple internet and social media platforms. You should invest as much as you can on content through any channels that you can find.

You can do this by putting out a lot of content on your website, video sharing sites, and even online forums. Make sure that some of your content is educational and informative. Don't just focus on content that is meant to increase sells.

Sometimes, people appreciate it more when you create content just to teach them the ins and outs of your business. For example, you can create a video series that explains how a microbrewery operates by taking the viewers on a journey through your facilities.

Videos like these can make viewers feel like they know your brand intimately, and this will make them more inclined to become regular customers.

Chapter 8: Common Mistakes Even Experienced Brewers Make That Can Run You Out of Business

When running a microbrewery, it's easy to make certain mistakes that could irreparably ruin your business. In this chapter, I will discuss the most common and the fatal mistakes microbrewers make that you'll want to avoid. Here are the mistakes that you should avoid at all costs:

Giving up controlling interest to another person or entity

When you are running a microbrewery, you are sort of an artist, which means that the craft should take center stage, and you shouldn't just be driven by the desire to maximize profit. If you give up control of your microbrewery to someone who doesn't understand that, then you will never have the freedom and the autonomy to practice your craft.

This is a mistake that even seasoned microbrewers have done at some point. When they are looking to expand, and they need some more investment, some have gone on to bring on investors who only care about profit, and that has ended up causing these breweries to pretty much lose their identities.

No matter how desperate you are for funding, don't let someone else be the boss of you. The micro-brewing model only works when you are the boss, and you make all the final decisions concerning the product.

It's okay to consult experts when it comes to branding or marketing, but you are the "chef." Letting go of that means that you are back to being just a regular guy with a day job.

Failing to protect intellectual property

There are three types of intellectual properties that microbreweries need to take steps to protect if they want to avoid issues in the future. The first are trademarks, which are words or images that represent your business or your product.

The second type is copyrights, which are fixed works of art that require some level of creativity to come up with. The third type is trade secrets, which refer to things that have value, and are likely to lose that value if they were to be made public.

Many brewers make the mistake of failing to understand the importance of these intellectual properties, and they, therefore, fail to take steps to secure them. If you have designed a great logo for your microbrewery or one of your beers, you should immediately file with the USPTO to prevent anyone else from using your trademark.

If you have come up with say any copyrightable content, perhaps the kind you are using to market your microbrewery, make sure that you copyright it to keep anyone else from copying it (this includes the information you publish on your website because some competitors may decide to just copy-paste your content instead of creating their own).

Remember to move as fast as possible to trademark your unique designs and names, because there are scammers who deliberately copy people's IP before they are able to secure them just so that they can sue you later on and settle out of court. This is more common with patents, but it still happens with trademarks.

For example, if you launch a new beer with a nice logo before you file the paperwork with the USPTO, someone could copy your logo, modify it a little bit, and then file the paperwork before you (there will be some conflict even if it's for a completely different product).

Since you would have already spent money promoting that logo, you may feel obligated to just settle with the scammer. If you can't afford to settle, you might be forced to rebrand, and that could sink your business.

When it comes to trade secrets, there are no formal legal procedures that can enable you to protect them. Even though the law provides some forms of recourse if someone steals your trade secrets, it would be extremely difficult for you to prove that they did.

The best option for you is to guard your trade secrets as closely as possible.

Many microbrewers fail to protect their beer recipes and formulas, which are essentially trade secrets. It's very difficult to come up with great beer recipes, and you would probably have to experiment with lots of batches over many months or even years to come up with a few that customers really seem to enjoy.

When you find these recipes, make sure that you guard them closely. If you make a beer that becomes a great hit and you let everyone know what went into the process, a few months down the line, a handful of your competitors will have beers that taste exactly like yours, and you will lose your edge in the market.

Failing to adapt your business plan to changing circumstances

You may have a great business plan at the beginning, and you may execute that plan with precision until you build a successful microbrewery, but then what's next? Many brewers tend to assume that once things are off the ground, they no longer need a business plan, but that is when things go wrong.

You always need to have a plan in place. You can't just wing it. If you outgrow your business plan, you should create another one that captures your new circumstances, one that lays out a new vision for your company.

Even if your business plan is working great, and it's helping you accomplish everything that you had set out to accomplish, you need to understand that circumstances change. Things evolve in the micro-brewing industry very fast.

Online marketing platforms rise and fall every day, so you need to be ready to adjust your plan to keep it viable. If new trends in micro-brewing are emerging, don't stick with your old plan just because it's still bringing in the cash at the moment.

Set aside a portion of your budget to develop new marketing angles and make it your business to know everything that is going on in the industry. The marketing strategy that you have laid out in your business plan could be working just fine, but what if someone comes up with a new social media platform, and all the "cool kids" start using it?

You should be on the lookout for changes like that so you can adapt and evolve because if you don't, your microbrewery could go out of business.

Hiring the wrong employees

The success of a microbrewery depends on the quality of the workers that it has. In the beginning, when you are strapped for cash, you might want to hire unskilled people because you don't have to pay them as much money, but that is a mistake.

Make sure that the people you hire have the right qualifications, and they understand the chemistry involved in the brewing process. You should also make sure that they have the proper training on matters such as food safety.

You also want to avoid hiring people who want to work for you for the wrong reason. Someone might look for a job at your microbrewery because they want to learn your recipes, quit, and start a brewery of their own.

There is nothing wrong with hiring someone who wants to learn the business from you (if you find an employee who has a real passion for brewing, then you should consider yourself lucky), but you want to keep an eye out for the "corporate espionage" types.

There are also some people who look for jobs in the brewing industry because they have this mentality that working in a brewery means they get to drink free booze throughout the day!

You should learn to screen for people like that, and you should have a "no sampling the product" rule (of course, someone has to taste the final product for quality control purposes, just make sure it's nothing more than that).

Making deals without legal representation

Whether you are getting started, or you have been running your microbrewery for a while, you will realize that part of your job is to strike all sorts of deals with suppliers, distributors, and direct buyers.

This means that you will be signing contracts on a regular basis, and at some point, you will be tempted to just sign a deal without letting your lawyer take a look at it. Don't ever assume that a contract is "standard."

Unless you are the one providing it, make sure that you get clearance from your attorney before you sign anything.

Even if the terms of the contract seem fair and harmless, you have to understand that there are laws at play, and if anything in the contract contradicts any law, that contract could be null and void, and that could leave you exposed to a lot of liability.

If a contract has lots of numbers and figures on it, you might also want to let your accountant look at it to make sure that everything adds up.

Failing to get all the right insurance packages

We have mentioned that when you are running a microbrewery, you will need many different kinds of insurance coverages because you are exposed to liabilities which vary in nature. There are some types of coverage that are legally mandated, so it's unlikely that you could even be permitted to stay operational without those (for example, you can't do without health insurance for your employees).

However, many microbrewers make the mistake of overlooking some of the elective forms of insurance, which puts them at the risk of losing their businesses if things go sideways.

You have to make sure that you have everything covered under one or more policies so that no matter what happens, there is a way to pay for it. One mistake brewers make is that when they buy new equipment to add to the brewery, they can sometimes fail to add the new equipment to the policies that they have (or they may put off updating the paperwork).

Make sure that the moment you acquire new equipment for your brewery, you update your policy to reflect that new acquisition. It is almost impossible to self-insure your microbrewery because the potential for liability surpasses the potential for profitability.

If you can't afford all the premiums for the elective insurance policies, at the very least, make sure that your personal assets are secured from liability.

Violating labor laws

When you are trying to save on labor costs and to reduce your tax obligation, you might be tempted to misclassify some of your workers. Some microbreweries make the mistake of classifying their employees as independent contractors to get around labor laws, but this can be very risky because it's a violation of labor laws.

If you are reported for doing such a thing, you could be investigated by the state and federal governments, and you could be liable to pay fines and to compensate your workers. Be extremely careful about how you treat the people who work for you.

Another issue with your workers could arise if you are short on cash because of changes in market conditions, and then you feel the need to instigate a deferred wage policy. The problem here is that deferring someone's wage is only legal if they agree to it, you can't just impose a deferred wage policy without ending up in legal jeopardy.

The safe bet for you is to always plan ahead. Don't count on the current sales to pay your employees for that month. You should always have cash reserves to compensate your employees for at least the next three months or so, and if that's not possible, you should find ways to restructure things without violating any contractual obligations.

Buying brewing equipment from unknown manufacturers

You will be looking for affordable brewing equipment, whether you are getting started, you are looking to expand your operations, or you are replacing old tanks.

As you do your research, you may come across cheap equipment from unknown companies in foreign countries, and you may be tempted to buy them. The problem with this is that you won't be certain about the quality of that equipment.

The other issue is that you won't know for sure if spare parts for the equipment are readily available should you need some in the future.

Some brewers have sunk large sums of money into brewing equipment only to find that it is defective. Make sure you buy equipment from a reliable manufacturer or at least one that you can contact in case something goes wrong.

Conclusion

Thank you for making it through to the end of *How to Start a Microbrewery: Be Your Own Boss, Make Good Money, and Craft Beer That You and Others Love*, I hope it was informative and able to provide you with all of the tools you need to achieve your dream of starting your own microbrewery or brewpub.

The next step is to decide whether you finally want to get started on making that dream a reality. As I have stated time and time again, it all comes down to having a well thought out plan, so don't be in a rush.

Take a step back, think things through, and draft a comprehensive business plan. You should also start experimenting with different beer recipes and try to come up with the one that you believe is going to be liquid gold.

Remember that even if you have a great plan to begin with, some curveballs are going to be thrown in your direction, so be prepared for them. Don't be the kind of person that gives up at the first sight of adversity.

The most successful microbrewers are those who keep trying over and over until they arrive upon the right recipe, and until they get to the product that customers really love.

Also, remember to have fun! As a brewer, your job is literally to bring joy to your customers, so don't stress over the challenges that you encounter along the way.

No matter how much administrative work you have to deal with, remember that ultimately, what you are doing is creating a craft beer that people are going to love. Don't lock yourself in the office with the paperwork. You too deserve to enjoy your beer!

Finally, if you found this book useful in any way, leaving a review is always appreciated! Many thanks in advance!

Printed in Great Britain
by Amazon